Psychism and the Unconscious Mind

The peculiar diffomena, including telepathy, whole range of paranormal i their acceptance by the s time, popular interest in all such phenomena has burgeoned during the past few decades, often resulting in a too credulous attitude or, through ignorance of the rationale involved, in psychic damage to the individual. What has been critically needed has been that rare union of open mindedness and objective approach with the application of disciplined scientific methods. This book is the result of just such a union.

For a number of years a group of distinguished British scientists have devoted much time and applied the training of their various disciplines to an unprejudiced investigation of the many areas involved in psychic manifestations. Comments and discussions by individuals in this group on such subjects as telepathy, clairvoyance, hypnosis, the effects of mind-expanding drugs, the human aura, and related subjects, have been brought together in this unique volume. Because the writers are also students of Theosophy and Eastern philosophy, they have been able to add valuable insights to their considerations of the various phenomena without in any way lessening their objective scientific approach to this still mysterious field of human experience.

Psychism and the Unconscious Mind

COLLECTED ARTICLES FROM THE
SCIENCE GROUP OF THE
THEOSOPHICAL RESEARCH CENTRE
LONDON

Edited by
H. TUDOR EDMUNDS, M.B., B.S., M.R.C.S., L.R.C.P.
Chairman of the T.R.C. Science Group, London

A QUEST BOOK
Published under a grant from The Kern Foundation

THE THEOSOPHICAL PUBLISHING HOUSE
Wheaton, Ill., U.S.A.
Madras, India   London, England

© Theosophical Research Centre, 1968

First Quest edition, 1968
Second Quest edition, 1974

ISBN: 0-8356-0412-8

PRINTED IN THE UNITED STATES OF AMERICA

The articles in this volume are based on contributions made by:

Laurence J. Bendit, M.A., M.D., B.Ch., M.R.C.S., L.R.C.P., D.P.M.

Phoebe D. Bendit

H. Tudor Edmunds, M.B., B.S., M.R.C.S., L.R.C.P.

Arthur J. Ellison, B.Sc.(Eng.), C.Eng., M.I.Mech.E., F.I.E.E., Sen.Mem.I.E.E.E.

Roderick W. Grant, M.B., B.S., M.R.C.S., L.R.C.P.

Hugh S. Murdock, M.Sc., Ph.D.

Forbes G. Perry, C.Eng., A.M.I.Mech.E., A.F.R.Ae.S.

Hugh Shearman, Ph.D.

E. Lester Smith, D.Sc., F.R.I.C., F.R.S.

Corona G. Trew, Ph.D., D.Sc.

Harold Tyrwhitt

K. B. Wakelam

A. Withall

Contents

Foreword

In 1918 a few members of the Theosophical Society in England formed a Science Research Group, and when in 1934 the Theosophical Research Centre was inaugurated, this group became part of it. Its purpose was to examine theosophical teachings from a scientific viewpoint, and publish articles and transactions from time to time. Since then the group has met continuously, apart from the war years, and in 1957 it was decided to publish a *Science Group Journal* for the use of members. As time went on others became interested in the *Journal*, and its circulation increased to about three hundred, with subscribers in numerous countries. The present transaction comprises a first selection of articles and relevant correspondence from the *Science Group Journal* which seem to merit wider circulation. Some new material has also been added where it was thought further elaboration was desirable.

Because a number of minor alterations were needed, the author's names have been omitted from their respective articles; these nevertheless represent individual expressions of opinion, with which other contributors would not necessarily agree. The material is put forward in no dogmatic sense, but in the hope that the reader himself will enter into the discussion.

We should like to express our gratitude to Mr. V. Wallace Slater for his help in reading and commenting upon the rough draft; to Dr. Lester Smith, who has spent many hours in helping with the editing; and to all those other members of the Science Group who have assisted in various ways. We are particularly indebted to Mrs. Marian E. Ellison. Lastly, our thanks are due to Miss M. F. Billing- hurst, Miss Margaret Cannon, Miss Josephine Chase, Miss W. Marshall and Mrs. L. G. Murphey, who have kindly made our task easier by helping with the typing.

H. TUDOR EDMUNDS
(Editor)

Introduction

Theosophical textbooks written around the turn of the century described in detail an orderly range of psychic faculties. These statements were said to represent revealed truth, taken, in part at least, from ancient Sanskrit writings, and confirmed by the personal experience of the writers, notably Annie Besant and C. W. Leadbeater.

It may be recalled that the scientific theories of this era similarly tended towards an air of finality. But in both areas later work has rudely shaken this feeling of satisfaction. In physics especially, the discovery of a host of sub-atomic particles has demolished earlier theories, leaving a relatively fluid situation, with new hypotheses advanced in tentative fashion and an overall synthesis still awaited. It is not generally recognised that clairvoyant investigators were actually the first to suggest that the chemical atoms contain highly energetic smaller particles of various sizes.

In astronomy, too, the more recent discoveries of radio stars and quasars has thrown into disarray earlier theories of the nature of the universe, and several new theories are battling for acceptance.

In much the same way, advances in psychology and psychical research have thrown doubt on earlier explanations of the nature of psychic faculties. Other experienced psychics have not fully confirmed the observations of Besant and Leadbeater, but modern work cannot be said to have either confirmed or destroyed their theories; rather it has proceeded along different lines. However, it does throw grave doubts on the reliability of information gained by psychic means.

The 'classical' theosophical account of man and his latent powers must be briefly summarised in this introduction, though some aspects will be discussed in more detail later. Man is supposed to have subtler bodies interpenetrating the physical; the first three are the etheric, the astral or emotional, and the mental vehicles of consciousness, each existing on a plane of its own nature.

The theosophical literature describes prominent centres of the astral and mental bodies as chakras or wheels, but these are not themselves sense organs, though they are involved in psychic perceptivity. Instead, each subtle body has a kind of overall awareness of the corresponding plane, which, however, does not normally register in the physical waking consciousness. Before this can happen the etheric must be developed to act as a bridge between subtle and physical vehicles. This is done by 'awakening' the corresponding etheric chakras in turn; each then opens up a channel to a particular physical sense organ. Thus the psychic perception may come to the seer as if through his eyes, ears or other senses, despite its evident non-physical quality. In this way the psychic gains objective awareness of the higher levels, in distinction to the subjective awareness we all have through feeling and thinking.

Psychic faculties can be classified in various ways; the first subdivision that must be mentioned is into positive and negative psychism. The natural psychism of some animals and relatively primitive people is of the negative type, which is said to be associated with the sympathetic nervous system, whereas positive psychism operates via the cerebro-spinal system. The negative type is spontaneous and un-controlled, though it can be encouraged, as for example, by mediums 'sitting for development'. It requires a relaxed receptive mind, and advantageously a state of autohypnosis or light trance; but reception is not thus guaranteed; it is rather a state of openness to take what, if anything, comes along. The positive variety, on the contrary, operates with the mind fully alert, is always available and can be directed at will just like the physical senses, except that its scope is greater. Theosophical textbooks state further that these powers can be attained only by long-continued meditation and Raja Yoga practices, and preferably with the assistance of a teacher. The few people who have such faculties are disinclined to mention the fact or to use them idly, for they are regarded as incidental to self-training for the saintly life. Such individuals would be unlikely to offer themselves for testing by bodies like the Society for Psychical Research; it follows therefore that almost all such investigations have been upon less-competent psychics. However, this sub-division is not clear-cut, a fact which the early writers admitted and which has since become much clearer. It is said that the negative psychism tends to disappear as the intellect develops, but there are many highly intelligent people who experience slight or occasional psychic glimpses, and they do not seem to fit clearly into either category.

The faculties may be subdivided in other ways, but some of these have little real meaning. Such terms as 'clair-audience', 'clairvoyance' and 'clairsentience' refer only to the channels through which the general awareness at higher levels presents itself to the mind. Non-physical odours may sometimes be perceived, while a common experience of occasional psychics is for information to present itself directly to the mind. This last is often due to telepathy—a faculty hardly mentioned in the older books—but at other times there is no evident human source. Then deliberate clairvoyance can operate in space and in time; that is to say, attention can be focused upon a present event, at a distance, or upon one in the past, or sometimes even in the future. Psychometry may assist these more difficult feats; that is to say, some object associated with the desired vision is presented to the psychic as a link. Telescopic and microscopic vision is also said to be available to the trained psychic, or what is described in old Sanskrit writings as the ability to make oneself large or small at will (in consciousness).

The minor faculty of etheric sight remains to be mentioned. The etheric is the least rarefied of the superphysical levels, and can be seen by the etheric part of the physical eye, or so it is claimed. In its fully developed form, which seems to be rare, one can see through physical objects as through a mist; but many people claim to have incipient etheric sight and to see the human etheric aura and 'vitality globules' which are supposed to be etheric particles in the air.

Modern psychical researchers working in universities and elsewhere, and studying what they call 'extra-sensory perception' (E.S.P.), have tended to concentrate on telepathy. The reason is that this is readily amenable to planned experimentation, whereas other forms of psychism are not, and because many ordinary people have this faculty to a slight and unreliable degree. By myriads of trials with Zener cards they have proved beyond reasonable doubt that telepathy is a reality, which must be accepted, however difficult it may be to fit in with current theories of psychology. There remains, however, great reluctance to go any further, so that it is fashionable to explain any psychic perception in terms of telepathy, even when clairvoyance, for example, appears more plausible to the unbiased observer.

It must be pointed out that Besant, Leadbeater and other early writers frequently stressed the fallibility of information gleaned psychically; modern psychology has so strongly underlined this warning as to shake one's faith in any psychic investigations. After all, even the physical senses are easily fooled, experienced though we are in their use. Nor do we realise the extent to which we unconsciously interpret sense data by reference to memories and logical thinking before we accept them. Anyone who gains psychic perceptivity is like one born blind who suddenly gains sight through an operation. His initial sight of a world of colour and movement, devoid of perspective or correlation with other senses, is terrifying and bewildering. The psychic similarly has no frame of reference or bases for comparison, and is at a loss how to express his strange visions in words. It must be emphasised that these visions do not automatically convey any explanation of their own nature. Nor, of course, does physical vision, except in so far as we add explanations unconsciously from previous experience. Understanding *may* be vouchsafed in addition, but if so that is due to the operation of a quite different faculty, that of intuition. The early theosophical writers spoke of the distortions caused to psychic visions by the personality, on their way through to the physical brain. The modern psychologist speaks of unconscious dramatisation by the subconscious mind. The effect is much the same; imagination and unwarranted interpretations are superimposed upon the perception until the product often has little residual significance. Intelligent psychics recognise this, at least in respect of the work of other psychics; but they usually seem to have complete faith in their own observations.

Consideration of all this embroidery brings some of our

contributors to almost total rejection of the validity of psychic investigations; others feel it may be worth while trying to discern the ground pattern beneath it.

We were fortunate in having available for study two investigations by a highly experienced positive psychic, Mr. Geoffrey Hodson. In the first, the seer probed into the interior of molecules and atoms by the technique of magnifying clairvoyance. This work is considered too technical for inclusion in the present transaction, though it is hoped that it can be published separately. Here we shall only mention that no close correlation with orthodox atomic structures appeared. We incline to the view that these discrepancies can be explained fairly simply. It seems doubtful whether this faculty permits the seer to observe physical matter at all; it seems more likely that he sees the etheric and astral 'counterparts' of the atoms, which could be very different from the physical subatomic structures. The second investigation used clairvoyance in time, and psychometry to examine fossil bones of primitive man. This fascinating investigation, made in collaboration with Mrs. M. E. Donnelly, is described in 'Fossils come to life', Section IV.

SECTION I

Psychical research

B

Clairvoyant research and some basic difficulties

The main difficulties with clairvoyance as a research tool are that we do not understand how it works, and we simply do not know how much to believe of what the clairvoyant tells us. To say this is by no means to impute dishonesty. We are not here concerned with clairvoyants of the fortune-telling type, who may not be beyond giving deliberate rein to imagination when their powers wane. Discussion of the special contributions of the few experienced psychics who have worked with the Theosophical Society will be deferred. There are other clairvoyants of limited or sporadic ability, who cherish the naïve belief that if they 'see' something it must be true. In this they are honest, but mistaken. The investigator who appreciates how misleading even the normal senses can often be will be highly mistrustful of testimony gained by relatively untried extra-sensory means. It *may* be true, so it would be unscientific to reject the whole of it out of hand. It is perhaps more likely to be false, for, as other contributors have explained, the dramatising ability of the unconscious mind can provide convincing visions. The trouble is that there seems little to guide either the psychic himself or the investigator in distinguishing reality from illusion. Repetition of the experience by the same psychic or others should not automatically convey greater conviction; the same falsifying factor may be at work all the time. When the vision concerns the supernormal it is also not easy to apply common-sense attitudes towards the evidence, such as to consider its general reasonableness and conformity with known facts. In such instances therefore the scales are weighted in favour of rejection, or at least of suspended judgement.

Moreover, among academic parapsychologists it is now fashionable to dispute clairvoyance as a mode of extra-sensory perception. The vast amount of spontaneous and experimental experience of clairvoyance is set aside in favour of telepathy, even if it has to be precognitive telepathy, as an explanation. Three kinds of telepathy can be distinguished, at least in theory. Postcognitive telepathy means obtaining information of some past event from the subconscious mind of another person, who may himself have forgotten it. This is telepathy of the past. In the normal kind of telepathy of the present the subject gets the conscious thoughts of another, who may or may not be making a deliberate effort to transmit them; even then it is possible that the thought has to slip into the unconscious before transfer can occur. Then there is precognitive telepathy, or telepathy of the future, in which thoughts are picked up before they are in anyone else's mind. Finally, precognition is foreknowledge of the future, with no implications as to mechanism. If the hypothesis of precognitive telepathy has to be accepted, then it would appear that there is no possibility of gaining any new information by psychic means, except, rather curiously, about the future. This seems an improbable restriction, to say the least; but unless clairvoyance can be re-established as a genuine faculty, the precognitive telepathy hypothesis will be used by critics to cast doubt on all clairvoyant research.

It might seem relatively easy to resolve these matters by discussion and experimentation with one or more psychics. In fact, it is not easy at all, and all the Science Group has achieved so far is a better understanding of what the problems are.

Nature of the problem

The first necessity is to think out what exactly we hope to discover, and how much it is feasible to achieve by stringent experimental techniques. Telepathy need not concern us; it has been established as an extra-sensory faculty with a certainty that should convince any scientist who cares to study the evidence; it is rarely useful as a research tool because it cannot give access to new knowledge—by definition it can provide only what is in someone's conscious or unconscious mind already. To express it in the broadest terms, our interest is to establish with certainty whether E.S.P. can operate through any channels other than telepathy. Many people regard clairvoyance as an already established faculty, but as mentioned, this has been thrown into doubt by the hypothesis of precognitive telepathy. Whether or not any such faculty exists, the term itself is a thoroughly unsatisfactory one, because it conveys the unwarranted implication that the mechanism is already understood, i.e. that it is indeed possible to obtain, telepathically, information that will be in another person's mind at some future time. For that matter, the old term clairvoyance—clear-seeing—is equally open to criticism. What is perceived is seldom entirely 'clear', nor is it 'seen' in any ordinary sense; the physical eyes are certainly not involved, and the term implies, perhaps falsely, some superphysical organ of vision. It certainly implies that the impression presents itself to the consciousness in visual guise; yet even this is not always so; J. B. Rhine (1), among others, has used the term clairvoyance to cover any information obtained extrasensorily that was not in anybody's mind at the time; it does not have to come in visual form, but may present itself directly as thought.

Some light has already been cast on these problems by individuals who do not regard themselves as psychics at all. These are people, students mostly, who have displayed E.S.P. abilities in some degree on testing, usually with the Zener cards bearing a range of five simple geometrical designs. Such subjects may distinguish the design on a card turned face-down, and may do this correctly sufficiently often in a long series of trials for the results to be entirely beyond explanation as chance occurrences (1). Such experiments already established, back in the 1930s, an extra-sensory faculty other than telepathy as usually understood, for the correct answer was not in any mind until after the call was made and the card turned up for checking. Such experiments did establish a second extra-sensory faculty, but nothing about its nature. It is playing a guessing game with words largely devoid of meaning to discuss whether this is clairvoyance or precognitive telepathy. Psychologists seem to think the mystery is lessened by calling it another kind of telepathy, however much common sense may rebel at the precognitive aspect—especially when card-guessing results can still come well above chance level when checking is deferred until the whole stack of twenty-five cards has been called. Moreover, it does not seem possible to devise any experiment to distinguish between the rival mechanisms, in respect of any particular extra-sensory event, because checking at once puts the knowledge into the investigator's mind.

Randomising machine

It *is* possible, however, to devise a randomising machine that could make this distinction in respect of a *series* of tests. The machine would present one of a known range of cards or objects behind an opaque screen, and the subject would record his impression by pressing the appropriate lever (or inserting a ball-bearing into the correspondingly labelled opening). The machine would finally present merely the total score of right and wrong answers, and no one would ever know to which individual trials they corresponded. It has been stated that some trials with such a machine gave no results significantly above chance expectation, but more work along these lines needs to be done. Negative results do not prove anything, the percipient may have been put off by the unfamiliar experimental conditions—a well-recognised occurrence. The wealth of recorded spontaneous clairvoyant experiences suggests that positive results are likely to be obtained under suitable conditions.

Positive results with such a machine would rule out normal or precognitive telepathy as a mechanism, and would establish an ability to acquire information from inanimate objects, a faculty that can be called clairvoyance provided we remember there is still no positive understanding of the mechanism; it would be known only that it did *not* involve tapping a human mind.

Over thirty years ago Rhine suggested there was really only one extra-sensory faculty, with minor variations. It might be regarded as a kind of reaching out by the sub-conscious mind to acquire information, either from living minds (telepathy) or from inanimate objects (clairvoyance). Rhine showed that most of his subjects had both faculties to the same degree; a good subject would score perhaps ten or eleven right out of twenty-five test cards either by 'pure clairvoyance' or by 'pure telepathy' from the agent's mental images (no cards being used). Both faculties functioned just as well at distances of hundreds of miles, with some subjects.

So if tests with a randomiser were positive, then something would have been achieved, but not really very much. Clairvoyance would be rehabilitated and precognitive telepathy proved not to be the mechanism in that particular trial. But it would still be impossible to prove that it *never* functions; indeed, there is so much testimony for spontaneous precognition that this probably has to be recognised as a genuine extra-sensory faculty (2, 3). So we should still be left wondering about the mechanism of other examples of 'clairvoyance'. Moreover, the experimental method can only be applied to naming hidden physical objects, yet this is seldom the situation in clairvoyant investigations; these are more often concerned with seeing events in the past (sometimes in the future), or descriptions of superphysical conditions, communications with discarnate entities and so on. The successful demonstration would do little to increase the credibility of visions like these to a sceptical scientist.

Positive and negative psychism

So far we have been discussing what the theosophists call negative psychism, which manifests spontaneously and sporadically. This ability is not under the subject's conscious control; the most he can do towards encouraging it is to empty the mind of all extraneous thoughts, maintain a recollection of the kind of information desired and a receptive attitude, and await what comes. It has been suggested that this is a vestigial psychism that was perhaps used by early man before he invented speech.

The situation is rather different, however, with the small group of highly experienced psychics who have worked in the Theosophical Society. Their powers were (or are) well developed and under deliberate conscious control, just like the normal sense organs. This is known as positive psychism and is regarded by some as a group of latent powers awaiting development by humanity in general, far in the future (4, 5). Moreover, these powers, the *siddhis* of Indian scriptures, seem more diverse than those manifested by negative psychics, including, for example, magnification that sometimes appears to be more powerful even than that of the electron microscope. The individuals concerned, for example, Annie Besant, C. W. Leadbeater, G. Hodson and Phoebe Bendit, are noteworthy for their scrupulous and fearless honesty, but in addition they have claimed to be well aware of the numerous pitfalls in psychic investigations, and have said that decades of experience had taught them to avoid being misled. They have fully admitted that some mistakes were nevertheless possible, and advancing scientific knowledge has shown that some were indeed made. Others doubtless remain undetected with certainty as yet, but much of their work would seem to merit qualified acceptance.

The doubt lingers, however, as to whether these individuals were so fully informed about sources of error as they sincerely believed. It is certainly true that psychologists of today know a lot about the unconscious mind that was unknown when much of this clairvoyant work was done; indeed, psychology was then hardly recognised as a branch of science. On the other hand, Besant and Leadbeater do seem to have been ahead of their time in their understanding of some aspects of the workings of the mind. Experienced psychics like Geoffrey Hodson say, if challenged, that they can readily distinguish a telepathic impression from a deliberately sought clairvoyant vision. Nevertheless, one is still left wondering whether even a highly experienced psychic can distinguish with certainty the source of extra-sensory information. It seems impossible to doubt that these psychic powers exist, but to what extent are the results embroidered or even vitiated by telepathy or unconscious dramatisation? These problems have been argued over for many years in the Science Group of the Theosophical Research Centre in London. It will be seen that the attitudes of contributors to this transaction range most of the way from total credence to total rejection of information gained by extra-sensory means.

Barriers to objective proof

It would be valuable if one of the experienced psychics would demonstrate his powers under test conditions. The problem was discussed at length with Geoffrey Hodson, but, even had he not been departing shortly for a lecture tour, he was disinclined to co-operate himself, as others have been. This attitude, though disappointing, is quite under-standable. Positive psychism is said to derive from the spiritual man (see Section II, 'Levels of consciousness'), i.e. the higher self or ego (in theosophical terminology). There-fore it cannot be operated effectively and free from distortion unless the ego is interested in the project. Trying to see the problem from his level, is it to be expected that he would be concerned to convince critics lacking in faith and spiritual perceptions? Indeed, is it ever possible to convince hardened sceptics? They would treat the psychic as they would a stage magician, and would prefer to admit failure to detect the trick than the validity of psychic powers.

The occult tradition that psychic powers must not be wasted or flaunted affords another reason for refusing to submit them to test; for the experienced psychic sincerely believes that no demonstration is necessary. His faculties were fully tested in years gone by to the satisfaction of himself and colleagues, though not indeed so stringently as they would be today. Then in the course of clairvoyant investigations additional tests cropped up inadvertently from time to time, which re-established his confidence. He can see no need for anything more, and desires only to apply his powers if possible to seek new knowledge or to assist in medical diagnosis, for example. He will select his projects with care for other personal reasons. It is not always realised that faultless exercise of positive psychism demands perfect health and tranquillity of body and mind; it involves intense concentration and keying up the psyche to a state of extreme sensitivity in which a sudden noise or *even a critical mental atmosphere* is as painful as a knife wound to a normal person (6). The work itself causes great strain and nervous exhaustion, so evidently is not to be undertaken lightly. Incidentally, this is another feature that distinguishes positive from negative psychism; the latter does not normally seem to be accompanied by any such strain. Notable exceptions are those rare occasions when a subject makes a supreme effort to achieve a high score; possibly indeed the accompanying strange and unwelcome nervous tension signifies a brief premature awakening of positive psychic powers.

A final factor that makes any psychic shrink from test conditions is the conscious or unconscious fear of failure. Such fears would themselves impede his powers. Unsuitable test conditions or a critical unsympathetic attitude on the part of the investigator could be the main causes of failure, but in any event this is a situation the psychic is loth to risk because it would sap his confidence in his own abilities.

This is probably why the best test results have come from normal subjects with no reputation to lose because they do not regard themselves as psychics. Since it seems unlikely that professed psychics will present themselves, it is pointless to enumerate the tests that have been devised.

It would be fitting to conclude by repeating the opening sentence of the article. Instead, let us confess our ignorance, and our inability to dispel it, in the words of the World Meteorological Organisation concerning weather forecasting: 'The basic characteristics of uncertainty will almost surely continue to be operationally significant for the foreseeable future.'

References

1. J. B. Rhine, *Extrasensory Perception*.
2. L. E. Rhine, *Hidden Channels of the Mind*
3. A. W. Osborn, *The Future Is Now*, University Books Inc., New York.
4. C. W. Leadbeater, *Clairvoyance*, The Theosophical Publishing House, London, 1908.
5. Phoebe Payne, *Man's Latent Powers*, Faber & Faber Ltd., London, 1938.
6. Phoebe Payne, *The Psychic Sense*, Faber & Faber Ltd., London.

Special problems in clairvoyant research

The previous article considered the problems from first principles, querying even whether clairvoyance can be recognised as a psychic faculty. In this one it will be accepted that the psychic does indeed deploy the powers he claims. This particular investigation, carried out in Australia by Geoffrey Hodson at the instigation of Dr. D. D. Lyness, concerns mainly observations by 'magnifying clairvoyance' of a conductor carrying electric current. The intention is to point out the exceptional difficulties of such investigations and of describing what is seen in meaningful terms; also the care that should be taken in planning and in devising suitable questions to guide the observer. It turns out that this particular investigation was ill-conceived in several respects.

For illustration, two short excerpts are first given, transcribed verbatim from the tape recordings.

G.H. Some carbon atoms are face to face, which gives me the impression of rather a jumble of atoms than any kind of regular arrangement or lattice in the terms of the physicist. However, that was a kind of glimpse I had when I was really watching the free, I'll call them anu, but I can't identify them wholly as such, which are all pervading within the rod of graphite and are in constant free motion (I have the current switched off as I am describing), and they seem to have no relationship whatever to the chemical atoms. Now I am switching on. I think the maximum current. At least I will in a minute when I get my sight clearer. Well, I can only repeat that a certain number of these free bodies are caught within an invisible force (I presume) which forces them, and I am using merely descriptive language, to lie flat so that those that are affected are now so to say, lateral, horizontal. H'm, one moment . . . it's a thin core.

D.D.L. Is there only one such core in the rod?

G.H. I can only see one, and it seems to run along the centre of it. I want to try and get a proportionate size. I am inclined to lose it when I look at the whole. No . . . I only see one, shall we say.

*

G.H. I am endeavouring to observe the phenomena produced by the electric current flowing through this graphite bar, and this morning my experiences have brought me to another but in no way different view of them. First, it seems that there are two distinct but, of course, intimately related happenings. One is on the surface and in the air surrounding the bar and going a little under it (the surface). It isn't with the vision I am using at the moment describable in terms of any lighted object. There must be, I presume, objects there, but it looks more like a colourless fluid, not fluidic, a force, a stream, a current of something more like wind if one could see it. Rushing, I feel I must say, racing from left to right as I look at this bar. This completely encloses the bar and extends at least half if not more of its thickness outside of it, and at present it seems (slightly only) below the surface. The other is the activity at the centre down the middle of the bar, which I called the core yesterday. Now it requires a slight shift of focus to get this. Not quite the simple phenomenon that I first began to see . . . today in addition to locked particles which I now think are anu, for a reason I will give in a moment, there are also moving bodies also travelling along the core. In fact, there's a . . . it's not a simple, but a very complex disturbance which is created by the current, however orderly it may be.

★

These descriptions are reminiscent of the reports of people blind from birth who suddenly acquire sight. They see a bewildering world of moving shapes and colours, totally unrelated at first with the reports from their other senses, or with any mental concepts; until practice is gained there is no ability to judge distances or relative sizes of near and far objects. We seldom appreciate how much selection and interpretation we apply in normal vision between retinal and mental images of a scene. The clairvoyant with his apparent power of magnification (or rather of 'making himself small at will'), entering in consciousness into a completely new world of subatomic dimensions, is understandably lost, like a newly sighted man. He 'sees' a maze of phenomena that defy description, the true nature of which he cannot know. For the occultist sees things that bear no labels, whereas the atomic physicist conversely names concepts he cannot see, some of which indeed *may* correspond with no objective physical particles, though of course they do correspond with observable events. How can we expect to correlate such diverse techniques? It is by no means certain, for example, that the electron is something a clairvoyant 'ought' to see; even if it were, it might be travelling too fast any-how.

In so far as they cover the same ground, Hodson's observations appear to tally with those of Besant and Leadbeater recorded in their book *Occult Chemistry*. These authors mentioned the rapid motions of all the particles they observed, which they believed to be subatomic, and stated that for detailed observation it was necessary to still this movement by an effort of will. The implication was that they could actually hold the atom and its contents stationary, presumably for some minutes. A more probable explanation is that they were able to 'make time stand still', as if by selecting a single frame from a ciné film for examination as a 'still'. Geoffrey Hodson has this same ability; he is not certain how it operates, but agreed in a later discussion that the second explanation seemed the more likely.

In work of this kind the clairvoyant is evidently operating under great strain, which must inevitably be increased when he is asked to try to focus simultaneously on things that differ in magnitude by a factor of 10^6 or even 10^{12}. Scaling-up to ordinary dimensions shows how exceedingly difficult if not impossible such a task must be; it has been truly said that few people have any clear concept of a million. Thus Hodson was several times asked to count the fundamental particles (called anu) in a chemical atom, and although he described getting inside an oxygen atom, he was unable to manage the counting. Elsewhere in this investigation it is recorded that Lyness (quoting *Occult Chemistry*) suggested, and Hodson confirmed, that this smallest particle is of the order of one-millionth the size of a chemical atom. If this is so, and refers to linear dimensions, then scaled-up counting is roughly equivalent to counting fast-flying gnats in a cubic mile of space! It is difficult to make a direct visual comparison of objects differing in size by a factor of 10^4 (1 mm and 10 metres). Probably most English people would do it by guessing the two sizes in fractions of an inch and feet, and applying mental arithmetic, instead of imagining one laid against the other 10,000 times. The clairvoyant can only attempt it this second way, so comparisons one or two orders of magnitude even wider apart seem impossible without some recognisable yardstick of intermediate size. One might suggest that the factor of a million was just a faulty guess in both sets of investigations.

Assessing the difficulty of the next experiment does not involve any such clairvoyant comparisons. When electric current was passing through a graphite rod Hodson observed strings of subatomic particles arranged head-to-tail, and also that these formations did not appear to occupy the entire cross-section of the conductor. When the current was altered (by a large factor) he was asked to assess the change in the proportion of the conductor so occupied. Now this must be somewhat akin to making a snap visual judgement of the density of traffic in Greater London at, say, 5 p.m. compared with 7 p.m., i.e. after the rush-hour. Even with visual aids like a telescope on an aeroplane this would be difficult. However, it would be a better analogy if the traffic were composed of ants instead of cars; also London, with all its streets and buildings, should be 20 miles *high* as well as that much across. The size ratio (about 3×10^7) is about the same as that between the $\frac{1}{8}$-inch conductor and a chemical atom (determined by physical means). However, Hodson was looking at the much smaller subatomic particles, making the exercise that much harder still.

Such comparisons are by no means obvious until one makes the calculations, and there is hardly time to do this when the queries crop up in response to something the psychic has said. They are included mainly to emphasise that clairvoyant powers should be sedulously conserved and used only after careful planning—much as one would with, say, a giant cyclotron costing £1000 an hour to run.

In later experiments Geoffrey Hodson was asked to determine by magnifying clairvoyance when current was flowing in the conductor, while the investigator turned a hidden switch on and off. He was unable to do this consistently. A suggested explanation was that he stilled or slowed the movement of the particles for observation, so that he continued to observe some past moment of time instead of the actual present moments when the current was switched. He confirmed that he remained inside the wire in consciousness during the entire experiment. However, a simpler explanation for the failure has since been suggested. Classical physics depicts a conductor as an assemblage of atoms with free electrons in vast numbers rushing about in all directions. When it carries a modest direct current the only effect is a tendency for some of the electrons to drift in one direction. If one could see electrons this drift would be scarcely noticeable, superimposed on the more intense random movement. The following analogy has been offered: 'In analogy, what he was trying to do was to stand in the middle of a busy pavement in London's Oxford Street and determine whether or not several unmarked pedestrians who had been instructed to walk past him (in the same direction and at the rate of about four pedestrians per hour perhaps) were actually doing so or not! These pedestrians represent the current-carrying electrons in the wire, and all the others represent the hundreds of amperes of non-current-carrying electrons

c

present in a metal.' Thus if Hodson saw electrons or particles
that behave similarly, then he could not be expected to discern whether or not current was flowing, and the experiment was not a fair test of clairvoyant abilities.

Some limitations of mediumship

Notes from a statement made by a member of the Science Group

Some years ago when I was investigating the phenomena of trance mediumship I went to a woman who had well-developed mediumistic powers, though she was of poor education, and asked her if she would allow me to investigate her clairvoyant abilities scientifically and take notes. She willingly agreed, so I went to her a number of times to make various tests. On the very first occasion she quickly went into a trance and her 'control', a so-called little Red Indian girl, was said to be in charge and spoke to me through her. (There is every reason to believe that this was simply a part of the medium's mind which was acting separately, as usually happens in trance mediumship, but this was unimportant to me, as I was only interested in the *content* of what she had to say, wherever it might be coming from.)

Almost at once, without my saying a word, she said, 'What have you been doing! . . . you must not do that, it is terribly dangerous! You must not mix the powders together!' And she went on to describe what another student and I had done recently in making some nitrogen iodide, the substance which is safe to handle when wet, but when dry will explode when touched even with a wisp of cotton-wool.

It so happens we were working in a laboratory, and were well aware of the need for care, and we made only a very small quantity, and divided it while wet into still smaller quantities, so that we took no risks. Later we tested its explodability by touching minute quantities with various articles. There was no danger, and no one was hurt. I realised then that the medium had the power of reading an unconscious part of my mind as the event was past, and I was not thinking about it during the session; but having read the facts, she then put *her* own interpretation on them, not mine.

I did numerous further experiments and found that in all the things she told me of myself and of other people, and things connected with me, she was practically 100% accurate. Her accuracy in trivialities that no one other than myself knew about because they were so unimportant was truly remarkable, and there was no doubt she was reading my mind and my memory, even when I was not then thinking about the things she mentioned. As a medium *she* was convinced that she got her information from somewhere else, not from me.

On one occasion she showed me it was possible to get in contact with some close friends of mine in South America. The link seemed to be made through my own conscious thoughts and mental images of them, and she described various things as happening at that moment in Buenos Aires —we were in Cardiff, the war was on and owing to sub-marine activities and censorship of letters, private correspondence was very unsatisfactory, and letters were often lost. The medium suddenly told me that one of the members of the South American family *was already sailing* in order to bring two young children to their mother here in England. The boat was described, and she stated that they would not come to the usual port on arrival here, but would go to a different one for reasons of safety, and would arrive in about five weeks. Now most of this was entirely unknown to me, and therefore she was not reading my mind on this occasion.

The five weeks went by and a further five before I discovered that my friends had not set out from Buenos Aires at all, so the whole thing seemed to be a fantasy. But still later I discovered that plans had been made in exactly the way the medium had described. The children were to be brought by their aunt to England in the boat described, etc., etc., but at the last moment the whole thing was cancelled, as it was considered too dangerous. It is obvious that much concentrated thought had been put into these plans by various people, and what the medium was apparently able to see was the well-developed thoughtforms, but she could not distinguish between a thoughtform and an accomplished fact. From her point of view, therefore, the error was a small one, since physical activity invariably follows planned thought, but from the physical plane point of view the error appeared to be tremendous.

These few experiments were sufficient to convince me that genuine mediums can sometimes show a remarkably high degree of accurate telepathy, reading the contents of peoples' minds whether or not they are thinking of the things the medium picks up. From these and other experiments it also seems that they can read the thoughts more easily than material facts.

This accounts for the limited value of the information usually given out by a medium although she may sincerely believe she is contacting some high spiritual source, for it will almost invariably be found that new information unknown to others practically never comes through, but is limited to the total contents of the medium's and sitter's minds.

Some new developments in psychical research

In recent times there has been a renewed interest in the use of hypnosis for psychical research. In many ways, one must be cautious in accepting evidence produced, and it is generally considered among experts in parapsychology that most attempts at the production of E.S.P. through hypnosis have failed. A factor often overlooked is our basic confusion as to the exact processes involved—for while a deep trance state puts the subconscious mind of the subject to the fore, consciousness is never lost; moreover, practitioners are not happy to make public, cases in which they have observed E.S.P. in action; it is too near to the 'lunatic fringe' of psychiatry, and might adversely affect their practice.

Meares in his *System of Medical Hypnosis* gives two examples of telepathy between himself and a subject, but adds that when next day he called in a hospital pathologist to act as witness, there was no success. He goes on to say that if telepathic communication does occur between patient and practitioner, then this carries a very grave responsibility, for the therapist must be very careful lest he think any negative thought that could act as a counter-suggestion.

Another issue that has been raised by Leslie LeCron concerns the frequency with which psychic phenomena were reported by mesmerists, who used a much longer and more complex technique; they did not, however, make use of controls (1). More recently Gurney and Podmore of the S.P.R. have had success in demonstrating subjects who felt pain when the hypnotist was pinched at some place on his body, and one operator who, by supposed telepathic suggestion, could cause one finger as designated to become anaesthetised (2). Janet and Richet were able to hypnotise a girl so as to exhibit what they term 'travelling clairvoyance', and once when mentally transported from Le Havre to Paris she reported that the laboratory owned by the researchers was burning down, which proved to be entirely correct.

It may well be shown one day that the modern methods of induction of hypnosis—which take 15–20 minutes—lack some vital procedure that the older practitioners made use of during their 1–5-hour stints of continuous induction with passes. The difference in timing alone suggests that there could be a necessary physiological change that takes hours rather than minutes to occur. If induction is extended over a yet longer period, either continuously or intermittently, some subjects will enter a much deeper state, termed a plenary trance. In the 1890s Wetterstrand, a Swedish physician, used to maintain such a trance in his patients for one, two or more weeks; some would reach a state of almost suspended animation. There was cessation of much bodily function, no nourishment was taken, and respiration and heart rates became greatly reduced (3). It may eventually be possible to achieve such states more quickly with the aid of hypnotic drugs and thereby a really convincing procedure whereby the isolation of pure subconscious activity could be achieved. Once these barriers have been broken through it would become legitimate to attempt regression and progression experiments, but as yet this is a very doubtful way of investigating pure subconscious activity.

Hypnosis does, however, have important contributions as

a tool for psychical researchers. For instance, in the sphere of telepathic research, the great French psychiatrist, Janet, has reported 16 successful attempts out of 22 to hypnotise at distances of at least 500 metres, the time for each trial having been randomly determined. In certain of these trials post-hypnotic suggestions were successfully conveyed as well (4). The Soviet physiologist, Vasiliev, has succeeded in hypnosis through two walls to a distant room (5), but as with Janet it is hard to be certain that the element of suggestion has been properly removed. If such experiments could be combined with an electric tracing that showed unequivocal changes when hypnosis supervened which *could not be self-induced by the subject*, then telepathy could be put on a really sound scientific basis that was not subject to the statisticians' application of a rule of probability.

Meanwhile, more insight is being gained into the nature of the telepathic state itself, and the sort of individuals who make exceptionally good subjects. Numerous psychiatrists hold the opinion that the paranoiac (*a*) is capable of utilising extra-sensory perception in his characteristically keen discernment of another's thoughts which refer to him (6). Ehrenwald goes further to suggest that the paranoiac is telepathically sensitive to the repressed sadistic-aggressive tendencies in the unconscious minds of his fellow men.

Ullman reports that he has often experienced paranormal ability in very ill individuals who are teetering on the brink of psychotic breakdown, but are not yet over the edge. He has even observed an increase in the scores of extra-sensory card tests of mental patients after electro-shock and insulin shock, and during narco-analysis (7). Hollos, a Hungarian psychoanalyst, reports 500 cases where telepathy has occurred between analyst and patient, and says that they are most frequent during a difficult period in the analyst's life. It appears to be related to the process of repression that goes on in the analyst's mind (8). This is also suggested by Ehrenwald's concept of 'doctrinal compliance', whereby much of what a therapist finds in the patient's mind is really material that has been telepathically implanted there by himself (9). Dr. Bendit has long propounded the belief that a sizeable proportion of mental patients suffer the interference of some psi function (10).

Pederson-Krag has gone even further, and suggests that human speech had to be invented because telepathic communication revealed too much of man's aggressive and erotic impulses (11). Fitzherbert believes that the amnesia (b) for the first few years of one's life may result from the free telepathic flow from mother to child; this has obvious social implications, and calls for fuller investigation (12).

Up to the present time the only real insight that has been gained into the subjective aspects of hypnosis has been derived from personal testimonies, which although of some value, cannot be regarded as being either satisfactory, or open to logical quantitative assessment. Pratt, who has recently made such a survey, concluded that we will have to try and use subjects who have greater powers of description (13). However, new discoveries enable us to look forward to an improvement in this situation.

In the *British Medical Journal* of 19th January 1963 there is a summary of the literature recently published on the newly discovered Pineal gland hormones. It has long been known to have a gonadotrophic (c) action, but only very recently has it been possible to isolate the actual hormones, and determine their structure. One of the three isolated has been termed A.G.T. for short, and has a structure very closely related to harmaline, the active agent in caapi, a potion of jungle vine which Peruvian Indians take to induce hallucinations and delusions, and which is derived from serotinin, another of the three hormones isolated. This provides an interesting link with adrenochrome and adrenolutin, which are end-products of adrenaline metabolism in the body, which are also linked chemically to serotonin and A.G.T., and which are known to be powerful hallucinogenic agents.

As we know, certain conditions of stress and strain favour the accumulation of these chemicals in the body, and reveals once again the horny question of whether the rough state of deprivation in which most of the great mystics lived produced partially or wholly hallucinogenic states, or alternatively whether there is a true mystical experience at the core of every so-called 'delusional hallucination'. Obviously the state of mind and discipline of the individual could make a vital difference, but the ultimate value of 'revealed Truth' may one day come into serious question. At any rate, psychical research does underline the great difficulty of conveying a crucial subjective experience in objective terms, even if these terms be of an abstract nature and aimed at evoking comprehension through a similar experience of the phenomenon or Truth that an individual has touched on.

The first steps into the new field of assessing the effects of drugs on the phenomena of psychical research are now going ahead. Brugmans has found that a subject who was accustomed to drinking alcohol achieved significantly higher scores when under the influence of a moderate quantity. The increased relaxation and passive state of mind appeared to improve the psi faculty (14). Cadoret has shown that dexe-drine and sodium amytal cause the scoring to fall off; he also found that extra-sensory perception bore no relation to changes in the D.C. potential on the body surface (15). Figar has demonstrated a relationship between telepathic communication and limb blood flowing in the percipient and subject (16). Thus there are hopes that we may build a bridge that can link physiological and biochemical mechanisms with E.S.P. phenomena.

Another concept that now often recurs in articles in this field is the relationship between 'states of altered perception' and E.S.P. phenomena. Schizophrenia (d) is basically an alteration in the patient's response to his perceptions (Oswald); a drug-induced hallucinogenic state differs from this in that the feeling of depression, worthlessness and wish to die so often observed may be related to a lack of sympathy on the part of the experimenter, while on the other hand the subject is at any time capable of resuming, at least momentarily, the reality of his actual environment before he slides again into a world of fantasy. Since perception determines the ego boundaries, the ego boundaries lose their ego feeling.

Eileen Garrett supports this point of view when she says that she does not consider the experience of clairvoyance as either abnormal or extra-sensory. She states that it is simply due to intensification and refinement of the activity of the five senses of touch, taste, smell, sight and hearing combined and carried to a higher pitch of awareness than most people ever reach. She is able to induce these states by careful control of the physiological mechanisms of her body, and is able to appreciate the phenomena of the clairvoyant state by means of all her senses. She also provides evidence which indicates that there are changes in her basal metabolic rate during the periods in which she is in a trance. From her personal observations of the phenomena of mediumship she concludes that her powers are related to physiological mechanisms in her body which are probably of an endocrine nature, and has also made the interesting observation that under lysergic acid (which is related to adrenochrome) she could easily produce a clairvoyant state which resembled that of the naturally occurring condition except that it was more intense and lasted much longer (17).

As we plunge the further limits of our being into what William James called 'an altogether other dimension of existence—name it the mystical region, or the super-natural region, whichever you choose', we might remember his comment:

> '. . . I will call this higher part of the universe by the name of God. We and God have business with each other; and in opening ourselves to His influence our deepest destiny is fulfilled.' (The Varieties of Religious Experience.)

References

1. 'Hypnosis in the Production of Psi Phenomena', Leslie LeCron, *International Journal of Parapsychology*.
2. *Proceedings of the Society for Psychical Research*, Vol. II, Gurney.
3. *Hypnosis and its Application to Practical Medicine*, Wetterstrand, Putnam, New York, 1897.
4. 'Janet', *Bull. de la Soc. de Psychologie de Paris 21*, 1886.
5. 'Research on Telepathy in Soviet Russia', Ryzl M., *Journal of Parapsychology*, 25, 1961.

6. 'Medical Implications of Parapsych.', Carroll B. Nash, *International Journal of Parapsychology*, V, No. 3.
7. 'The Nature of Psi Process, Ullma', *Journal of Parapsychology*, 12, 1948.
8. *Psychoanalysis and the Occult*, Devereux, Int. Univ. Press, 1951.
9. *Telepathy and Medical Psychology*, Ehrenwald, George Allen, 1947.
10. *Paranormal Cognition*, L. J. Bendit, Faber, 1943.
11. 'Telepathy and Repression', Pederson-Krag, *Psychoanalytic Quarterly*, 16, 1947.
12. 'E.S.P. in early Childhood', Fitzherbert, *International Journal of Parapsychology*, 3, 1961.
13. 'Methods of Evaluating Verbal Material', Pratt, *Journal of Parapsychology*, 1960.
14. *Telepathic Experiments at the Univ. of Groningen*, Brugmans, 1921.
15. 'The Effect of Amytal and Dexedrine on E.S.P. Performance', Cadoret, *Journal of Parapsychology*, 17, 1953.
16. 'The Application of Plethysmography to the Objective Study of E.S.P.', Figar, *J. of The Society for Psychical Research*, 40, 1959.
17. E. J. Garrett, *My Life*, 1939; *Awareness*, 1945; *Adventures in the Supernormal*, 1949.
    Mentioned in 'The Physiological Basis of Paranormal Phenomena' by Cedric Wilson in the *International Journal of Parapsychology*, Vol. IV, No. 2, 1962.

Glossary

(a) Paranoiac: a person suffering from paranoia, a mental disease characterised by delusions of persecution.

(b) Amnesia: loss of memory to a pathological degree.

(*c*) Gonadotrophic: having stimulant effect upon the gametes or reproductive cells.

(*d*) Schizophrenia: pathologically this has been defined as 'an altered state of perception' (Oswald), but clinically is recognised as being a state of dissociation of the emotional from the intellectual life.

A note by a clairvoyant on clairvoyant research

In the world of science much is learned from observation, and the scientist is accustomed to the fact that much of what he sees he does not understand. He knows that repeated experiments and observations are essential in order to establish scientific facts which can be demonstrated and the experiments repeated at will.

Few people fully understand that in using the psychic faculty of clairvoyance one is still using external observation and sees much which is not deciphered accurately; all such vision is personal, and the evidence of the physical senses can never be accepted as proof of ultimate reality. Neither can that of the psychic senses, for the latter, just like the former, are extremely useful servants but are dangerous to accept as conveyors of ultimate truths. The observations of science are always extending the field of research, but the psychic observations that are made are liable to many subtleties of error because there is no exact method for the human psyche through which these observations are made.

Extra-sensory perception is not a cut and dried thing, but in a certain way can be related mainly to the physical senses, and are then referred to as clairvoyance, clairaudience and psychometry. They represent perception of immediate events. Telepathy is different in so far as it represents perception through space, and precognition perception through time. Percepts obtained in the latter two groups may be visual, or auditory, and so link up with physical sense

perception, or they may be in the form of direct pure
cognition. For example: a friend of the writer related that
while he was resting, suddenly, without rhyme or reason,
a clear picture of a man's head and face came before him. He
wondered where the picture came from, whether from his
own mind or that of another person, but there being no
answer he dismissed the subject. A fortnight later he went
away for a weekend visit to a strange place and a strange
house. He did not know anyone who was staying in the
house or had ever stayed there, so that there was no connect-
ing link, but as his host came up to him he instantly recognised the strange face that had been projected as a vision
across his mind a fortnight before. The face was obviously
not a subjective image such as one sees in a day-dream. It
was the result of extra-sensory perception, but what kind of
perception? Was it direct clairvoyance, was it telepathy
from the host, or was it precognition of an event still to
come?

Clairvoyance *per se*—if there is such a thing as the pure
faculty—is generally looked upon as the most useful aspect
of E.S.P. for scientific observation, because one is supposed
to be looking directly at the object; but again there is a possible difficulty. If a number of people test their range of
physical sight by the ordinary use of the colour spectrum
they will be found to have appreciably different limits of
perception, depending upon the structure and functioning
of their eyes. The same conditions are equally true in the
psychic world, the difference in this case depending upon
the development and activity of their psychic mechanisms.
Therefore, it is not at all surprising that there is so much
divergence of vision, and that so many clairvoyants often
disagree in their descriptions of the same thing. It depends

upon what inner level they are focusing their sight, and what attracts their attention. One person will discover one aspect of an object, another quite a different aspect of the same object.

All this is common knowledge, but it emphasises the difficulty of finding enough people who are capable of sustained and steady vision, and who are ready to continue making the same observations under different conditions in order to establish an adequate consistency of findings which can be usefully used as an adjunct to other forms of experiment.

The trained clairvoyant often uses what is known as magnification of sight in order to observe a minute object. The principle involved seems to the clairvoyant to be the same as that of the microscope in which different objectives are used for different scales of size. This is, of course, an over-simplification as far as the human mechanism is concerned. The power to magnify is highly specialised and seems to be derived from a function of the higher mind, not of the personality. Further to this point, no two highly trained clairvoyants will use their mechanism in precisely the same way, or 'see' from exactly the same fine point of focus, even though they may fully coincide as to their findings. There is a very interesting demonstration on this individual factor in an observation of Mr. Geoffrey Hodson recorded in a lecture by Dr. D. D. Lyness, of New Zealand. In observing slides of cancerous growth, he got exactly the right results, but how?

If he had been looking at a live cancer, this would have been a direct and immediate observation. But a microscope specimen was apparently used as a focus through which he was able to look back in time and see what appeared to be

D

the conditions in the live body. Quite clearly the 'vital currents' would not still exist in the dead and embalmed specimen. This is one of the many problems of the clairvoyant who is asked to analyse and observe dead specimens.

From the point of view of psychical research another complication occurs, which is telepathy—the passing of one mind's knowledge to another. Place and distance do not affect this, but the conscious or unconscious tuning in of one mind to the other is important. This is why in all controlled experiments with clairvoyance great care is taken that nobody knows the nature of a given specimen. To be fool-proof it has to work in this sort of way: A. holds the key, B. gives out the specimen for observation by C., but does not know its nature. A. on the other hand does not know which specimen is being handed out, because he is not present. These precautions eliminate other faculties except precognitive telepathy.

A fact for both scientists and psychic observers to realise is that *clairvoyance does not necessarily give any clue to the meaning of the thing observed*. A first year medical student can look at a slide and describe its appearance, but until he has learned a great deal more he will not be able to identify the tissue or the morbid process in it. Experience is just as necessary for clairvoyant understanding, and intuition is also required. There are many people who are not clairvoyant but who have a well-developed intuition which makes them go far ahead of their contemporaries. Such men as Rutherford and Einstein had minds of this order. The best combination for any research worker is intuition, plus experience, plus a trained psychic mechanism which enables one to make the same observation under many different conditions. This is a far cry for most of us, whatever our line of discovery.

To some this may appear to be a somewhat negative attitude towards the use of clairvoyance used in investigations of a scientific nature. On the contrary, it is nothing of the kind; but extreme caution is necessary, and it must be realised that extra-sensory experience gives a partial and not a whole solution to any enquiry. However, used in conjunction with other methods of research, it can be extraordinarily useful and suggestive.

Psychic perceptivity

Psychism and the mind

Parapsychology uses all the powerful and proved methods of modern science: data are obtained, checked, collated, and theories formulated. These theories are tested by experiment and altered as necessary; science is a living, dynamic, growing thing. We have only to look around at our modern technological civilisation to see the results of the scientific method of studying nature.

In parapsychology we are at present still assembling data, checking, confirming—and thinking. Traditional theosophical hypotheses are very useful in trying to understand the facts of experience, some of which fit and some do not. Checked data which do not fit are leading to changes in the hypotheses. This is, in fact, most of the point of the second and third Objects of The Theosophical Society.

Some of the work of parapsychologists in various fields will now briefly be mentioned because it gives valuable information about how the mind behaves under various conditions. A fuller understanding of how the mind behaves could resolve many of our problems and emphasise how very misleading the psychic powers can be if not properly checked.

General background material—the unconscious

It is worth while considering first how supernormally acquired information (that is, information not derived through the physical senses) comes in to the waking consciousness. In a word, it comes from the 'unconscious' in its widest sense. The unconscious is a term used by psychologists to describe those areas of mental life beyond the level of the normal conscious mind. (There is not complete unanimity among psychologists in the use of the word 'unconscious' and the present explanation is certainly an oversimplification, but it will suffice.) The deeper levels of the mind are not really accessible, but other parts may be reached with the aid of relaxation, association, hypnosis, trances, drugs, or simply sleep. All memories are in the unconscious and the most recent may of course readily be acquired at will and included in the conscious mind for a time.

If one accepts as a reasonable hypothesis the classical theosophical ideas of the planes of nature (physical, astral, mental, buddhic, etc.) these regions beyond the physical are part of the content of the unconscious for most of us. When a psychic observes (clairvoyantly) or hears (clairaudiently) then it would appear that the supernormally acquired information emerges from the unconscious and is presented to the waking consciousness in a form interpreted as sight or hearing. One may consider that there is only one psychic sense, but the waking consciousness necessarily interprets its information in terms of the customary five senses. There is perhaps a difference shown here between psychic and non-psychic people. We all have intuitions, 'hunches', but in the rather vague forms of feeling or apparently direct knowing. Psychics have these more precisely in terms of all the senses. A psychic is perhaps a person with gates open to portions of the unconscious, and a mind and brain that interprets as described. The unconscious includes both 'higher' and 'lower' parts of ourselves. Great art comes into the world from the unconscious—and so do foolish dreams and fantasies.

Drugs

Mescalin and lysergic acid derivatives alter the body
chemistry and sometimes lead to 'mystical experiences' of a
deeper reality. The experiences seem to be similar—perhaps
because of similar changes in brain chemistry—to those
produced by long fasting and prayer. Aldous Huxley writes
of breaking down the reducing valve of the brain, leading to
experiences of 'Mind at Large'. The result of staring at a
light flashing at the alpha-rhythm (the lowest rate of variation of the idling electric currents flowing in the brain when
inactive), is often some very interesting experiences (also
described by Aldous Huxley).

Yoga and Zen

The traditional methods of Raja Yoga (and to some extent
of Hatha Yoga) and of Zen Buddhism, can occasionally lead
to somewhat similar experiences. In Raja Yoga the messages
of the senses are cut off; the mind is controlled and ultimately ceases its normal activity. In Zen the mind is stupe-
fied to a similar passive state by means of a koan; enlightenment may then result which can lead to the experiences of
Nirvana and Satori. On the way of Yoga, the siddhis (the
psychic powers) are said to arrive. These are said to number
clairvoyance, clairaudience, leaving the body at will, reading
thoughts, etc., and the aspirant is warned against them.

Sensory deprivation

Very interesting results are being obtained in experiments
carried out in the U.S.A. and the U.S.S.R. in preparing men
for space exploration. A man is put into a quiet room,
fitted with gloves and light-diffusing goggles and sometimes

floated (in water at blood temperature) so that he feels no pressures against his skin. In other words, he is arranged so that no messages are transmitted inwards from the five senses. Strange 'psychic experiences' often occur in quite a short time. Few people can stand 24 hours of sensory deprivation and the limit is so far something like 72 hours. The experiences obtained are somewhat similar to those produced as a result of yoga practices and similar also to those resulting from mediumistic development. Men under conditions of sensory deprivation sometimes feel as if they were floating up out of the body, hearing voices, seeing distant scenes, i.e. they experience clairvoyance and clair-audience, but whether these are 'genuine' psychic experiences or wholly imaginary has not yet been proved.

Hypnogogic and hypnopompic images

Panoramic scenes, faces, visions, observed by many people when just on the point of going to sleep or of waking up, are similar in many ways to the above. Here again, the experiences result from complete physical relaxation and suspension of thought.

All this work is throwing much light on how the mind behaves when its normally continuous stream of data from the senses is cut off.

Hypnotism

Hypnotism will now be considered in some detail because the results are very relevant to many branches of this subject. Hypnotism is, of course, now quite 'respectable' and there has existed for several years a British Medical Association Sub-Committee dealing with it. Parapsychologists have studied it in a full appreciation of its importance since long before The Society for Psychical Research was founded in 1882.

Hypnosis is a state of suggestibility in which the critical faculty of the conscious mind is partially or wholly in abeyance; suggestion can then be accepted (under certain conditions) and go straight to the unconscious. The hypnotic state can be brought about in a number of different ways and can then produce very remarkable results. It may not have been realised, but several of these ways have already just been given, only the word hypnosis was not used. Before mentioning some more ways, a case demonstrated on B.B.C. television will be briefly mentioned here.

A girl was hypnotised, given the suggestion that some rows of empty chairs in the studio would later be filled with people, and was then brought out of the trance. She observed the people, in accordance with the suggestion, and invited a man to step forward. This non-existent man (visible only to her) answered a number of questions she put to him, in a perfectly normal manner; he appeared to her vision in a photograph taken at that time of the empty chair in which she imagined him to be sitting. She invited him to step on to the platform of a weighing machine and stated his weight, the pointer reading zero, of course, to the vision of the rest of the audience. As the psychiatrist who arranged the programme remarked afterwards, the girl's unconscious mind would have been quite able to fill the Albert Hall with people. If the suggestion made to the subject under hypnosis had been that a person in a semi-transparent astral body would come into the studio and discuss his life in the next world with her, she would have had that experience.

This state of hypnosis can be brought about by someone else—if the subject co-operates, but rarely otherwise. Or it can be brought about by oneself, and is then called auto-hypnosis.

Auto-hypnosis

Auto-hypnosis can result from intense concentration or meditation; or by staring at a point of light, or at one's navel; or by sitting relaxed in a dim light in a spiritualistic developing circle; or by other methods. When a subject is in a hypnotic trance, interesting things begin to happen. *What they are depends upon the suggestions made.*

When the conscious critical part of the mind is in abeyance, partially asleep, the normally unconscious part is enabled to do unusual things. The unconscious mind will dramatise various experiences, often to the astonishment and delight of the conscious mind, i.e. of the subject; moreover, it will dramatise what is suggested—or expected, which is the same thing. The unconscious mind of the girl on television dramatised a room full of people because of her belief and expectation.

The unconscious will produce pseudo-details of past lives if the appropriate suggestions are given. It will do this quite independently of whether reincarnation is true or not. If the person in trance is a spiritualist and the expectation is of a spirit guide, then one will probably appear, i.e. so far as the spiritualist is concerned, clairvoyance and clairaudience have been developed.

If an earnest monk spends many hours on his knees, fasting, praying and concentrating, asking Christ to give him guidance, then it is quite probable that he will have the experience he so earnestly desires. It would prove to be much quicker, and certainly less uncomfortable, if he allowed someone else to hypnotise him by one of the well-known methods and suggest precisely the same thing; the unconscious would do the rest.

The traditional Raja Yoga practices can sometimes put one into a trance, a hypnotic trance, and one can then suggest to oneself what has been taught by the teacher; that, for example, it is possible to leave the body through a chakram —and one will have precisely that experience. Similarly, clairvoyance and clairaudience may be produced. The experience will be what the yogi expects, i.e. what he has been taught.

If the yogi has not been given any very definite teaching, then the unconscious mind (or rather, that part of it which the writer calls 'George' and Tyrrell called 'the scenery setter') will create all kinds of interesting experiences for him. If he is a theosophist and believes in astral and mental planes, subtle bodies and thought forms, and enters a light trance, then he may well have experiences of those matters. 'George' has all the material of the yogi's mind, everything that he has read and experienced, and probably the material of other minds as well, which he can use in his dramatisation. And those experiences he will have *whether or not* those planes and bodies, etc., really exist; the experience is not proof of their reality.

After death or during sleep 'the next world' is probably similarly dramatised by 'George'. It is very clear why it is said 'under every flower a serpent lies coiled', for the next world appears to be created for each person quite automatically, the motivating force being desire (conscious and unconscious), and the material being memories of the physical world. This next world will be common to groups of telepathically interlinked people.

The important factor in all this is as follows. What

'George' gives (the results of the psychic faculties) is not always true. *He is not giving a view of the physical world.* If George's E.S.P. is working well, then what he produces may be true. If it is not working too well at that time—or perhaps one should say, if he is unable to push up his information into the conscious—then he will dramatise fantasy. It is vital to check whenever possible, i.e. to *train* 'George'. These recent experiments have discovered some of his little tricks. 'George' often dramatises other people's thoughts and latent memories and very much dislikes his tricks of deception being uncovered in this way. It is he who makes some psychics so uneasy, so unwilling to *test* their perceptions against facts, to agree to scientific experiments. (Happily this is not true of all psychics. Several have been extremely helpful to the Science Group, and they deserve our gratitude.)

Secondary personalities

Secondary personalities can be formed in the unconscious by suggestion and in trance they can sometimes take over the bodily mechanism while the primary personality is quiescent. Such secondary personalities often prove, perhaps in the form of a 'guide' or 'control', the means of transferring veridical E.S.P. information, which may have been acquired from the sitter and dramatised to appear as if from a person in the next world, or, more rarely, it may be truly acquired from a person in the next world.

Healing

The following remarks are relevant to Christian Science, psychic healing, vital magnetic healing . . . the name does not matter very much. Hypnosis can be used to prevent pain: it is ideal for childbirth and increasingly used. It can be suggested to a good subject under hypnosis that he will feel no pain when a needle is driven into his arm and he will not. All kinds of aches and pains can be removed by hypnosis, but needless to say it would be very dangerous to remove them in this way, because if the cause is not found a much worse state may result later, or a disease might progress unhindered. However, something like 60% of all diseases for which people see their doctors are psychogenic, i.e. generated by thought. An example would be a digestive upset due to worry, with no physiological cause whatever. Such patients may sometimes be restored to health, as is well known to every doctor, by means of a bottle of coloured water and a strong suggestion that a cure will result; a cure would per- haps be instantaneous by hypnosis. It is highly likely that this is what happens many times in the practice of Christian Science. The sufferer reads *Science and Health* (the famous textbook by Mary Baker Eddy), concentrates on it, accepts the suggestions, and is healed. The cure is not a proof that the facts read are true, it is merely an indication that they have been *accepted* as true. This would apply also to psychic or vital magnetic healing. The statement above should be kept firmly in mind—that a majority of all disabilities are psychological in origin.

Training the E.S.P faculty by hypnosis

The March 1962 *Journal* of The Society for Psychical Research contained a description of a most important piece of work in parapsychology by Dr. Milan Ryzl, which is very relevant to our study of the mind and its knowledge of the physical world. Dr. Milan Ryzl trained a large number of ordinary people by hypnosis and made them into 'clairvoyants'. The success of the E.S.P. was checked as it developed and the result is not merely a matter of belief or fantasy as is the case with many so-called clairvoyants. As described in the report his best subject was ultimately able to hypnotise herself, then producing the necessary inhibition of thought for E.S.P., use the developed E.S.P. faculty and remember the result after returning to normal consciousness. This work is reviewed in more detail in 'Hypnosis and the unconscious' in Section VII.

Conclusion

It seems that we are on the verge of a tremendous surge forward in our knowledge of the mind, especially concerning all those parts of which we are not normally conscious in our ordinary waking life. Telepathy and precognition show that the unconscious mind transcends space and time. Psychokinesis appears to show that the mind can sometimes directly affect matter. We are finding the keys to that mind —to the greatest experiences of which humanity has knowledge, but we need to be extremely cautious at all times as to how we interpret the psychological phenomena we experience or observe in others.

It is important to emphasise, because otherwise there may well be misunderstanding, that because the word hypnosis was used in the suggested explanation of an experience such as that in which the Master appears to the devotee, *it is not at all suggested that the experience has no validity*. It has the utmost possible validity and importance, unaffected by the words we use to describe it.

We are slowly discovering the many ways by which the path may be opened up from the conscious mind to the infinity of life which we call God and which we all share.

All is one in the depths of the unconscious—or at the highest planes, if the classical theosophical terminology is preferred. The Master is there, however he is looked upon, however he is described; the important thing is surely that he exists. But all Life is One: He is not separate from oneself. This is perhaps another indication of the fact implied in the statement: 'I am a man, yet also God in man.'

The interior organ of perception

The chief problem exercising the minds of thoughtful people today is how to bring together into one system the two approaches to the universe possessed by man as he is at present constituted. On the one hand we have the objective formal and structural view of the world as presented to us by modern science. On the other, the inner world which we all know at first hand, in which we live, with a direct immediacy of personal experience and sense of reality.

This problem was dealt with in The Blavatsky Lecture given by Mr. Basil Howell to the Theosophical Society in 1960. Mr. Howell's title, *The Metaphysics of Experience* stressed the point that the new step forward for which the world is ready is one beyond the formal structural presentation of ordinary science, it is a *Meta*physics. Only some form of synthesis in depth, a kind of complete 'nature-mind' three-dimensional perception will provide a framework into which both aspects of reality can be fitted. Such a view will be neither world-denying, taking refuge in the idea that all the phenomenal world is illusion and only the spiritual realm is real, a misconception of the eastern word 'maya', nor will it be life denying in that it rejects the whole range of spiritual and aesthetic experience. Such an ultra materialist view as the latter would have no place in it for those realities which are, after all, the only ones we know at direct first hand experience. Man's complete experience requires a metaphysic which incorporates both aspects of reality and in so doing evokes that third factor of spiritual

E

comprehension in which the objective, scientific and
common-sense experience (the theoretic component of
knowledge, using Northrop's terminology) and the subjective, immediate and aesthetic experience, including the
whole range of spiritual perceptions (the aesthetic component of knowledge) are integrated into a totality which is
'past and future and distant realms, all brought to a focus in
a present moment of perception' as Mr. Howell has described it. As he said further, in his Blavatsky Lecture,
'experience is an organic whole, in which each part has
value only in the light of all the rest'.

In the system of Indian philosophy and metaphysics which
form the basis of much modern theosophy there is to be
found a most exact and comprehensive analysis of man's
interior organ of perception and a detailed knowledge
concerning the nature of the human mind. This analysis
throws light upon the curious duality of human perception
which has been outlined above. At first sight the objective
and rather categorical nature of the eastern metaphysical
insights concerning the nature of the mind may appear
somewhat alien to western students. A closer study of the
method, with its introspections and observations of mental
states and processes can, however, show that this is a scientific
method applied to the field of consciousness and mental
perceptions. There is furthermore increasing evidence that
certain western investigators into the deeper aspects of
human psychology in the field of extra-sensory perception
are arriving by modern western research techniques at a
point where the eastern science of the mind can illumine
their problems. Thus, among others, Dr. Thouless and
Dr. Soal working in the field of parapsychology and
Professor Northrop in the field of philosophy are moving

to a point very close to the eastern view. In the issue of *The Laboratory Bulletin* (*M and B Laboratory Bulletin*, Vol. IV No. 2, pp. 19–25, May 1960) of the chemical firm *May and Baker*, Dr. S. G. Soal, one of the contemporary experts in the field of extra-sensory perception, has given a summary of certain very conclusive recent experiments on telepathy and has discussed the mechanism which might explain them and other paranormal factors of consciousness. Dr. Soal presents an impressive volume of recent experimental evidence for telepathy and then shows that all purely physical and mechanistic explanations are inadequate as an explanation. Even an interpretation that telepathy depends upon some form of radio transmission is shown to break down. The only type of explanation which Dr. Soal considers to be possible is 'a line of enquiry based on the assumption that thoughts, mental images and sensations are non-spatial entities which exist in their own right and are not merely aspects of brain activity which necessarily perish with the brain itself'. Soal goes on to quote Bergson's theory that the brain is not the generator of consciousness but merely an instrument which inhibits or modifies its manifestation. It is a kind of filter which allows those types of thought and feeling useful for ordinary terrestrial experience to be experienced by the self. On this view events derived from the state of one brain could under certain conditions interact with those of another individual and so cause the second individual 'to have mental experiences which are correlated to those of A' (the first individual). For this to be the case, Soal points out it must be assumed that 'mental states such as sensations, images, etc., do not exist in physical space and are therefore not subject to the limitations imposed upon physical entities. We must further assume that the core of a human being is a non-material self or soul, which is capable of various types of conscious experience.'

Mind and brain relationship

It is significant that at least four elements may be detected in this view of mind and brain relationships. There is:

1. A mind, not in physical space, in which mental states occur.
2. A soul or self that is non-material and capable of types of conscious experience.
3. An ego-focus associated with the brain and normal consciousness and indeed closely linked to the selective power of the brain.
4. Images and sensations and feelings which are the mental states of experience.

This work has been considered in some detail because of the very close approach it makes from the experimental and scientific angle to the eastern metaphysical analysis of the nature of the mind which will be found in theosophical literature. This is drawn from the knowledge of man and his mind taught in the different eastern metaphysical and philosophic schools. In these systems, detailed and elaborate analyses have been made of the nature of mind, of mental states and images and of the various insights or 'darsanas' by which the mind gains its perceptions. In *The Web of the Universe* and *The Play of Consciousness* by E. L. Gardner we have another theosophical attempt to study this deep inner field of perception and the nature of the human mind and its states in relation to brain and body from a viewpoint which combines both the eastern and the scientific standpoints.

One of the clearest eastern analyses of the nature of the mind as the inner organ of perception is that in Sri Shankara-charya's *Vivekachudamani*, translated as *The Crest Jewel of Discrimination or Wisdom*. Thus in Charles Johnson's translation of this work (Quarterly Book Department, New York, 1925) we find the following analysis of the mind:

'The mind formed vesture is formed of the powers of perception and the mind (manas); it is the cause of the distinction between the notions of "mine" and I, it is active in making a distinction of names and numbers; as more potent it pervades and dominates the former vesture (the vital or etheric body)' (Verse 171).

In another passage we find:

'Its (the mind vesture's) interior powers are called mind (Manas) intelligence (Buddhi), the personal sense (Ahan-kara) and imagination (Chitta), with their activities. The function of mind is the gathering together and separating of impulses; the function of intelligence is to reach a judgment regarding what is perceived. The function of the personal sense is the thought of "I" through the attribution of self-hood; the function of imagination is to hold the consciousness steady on its object' (Verse 95).

Other translators both eastern and western bring out slightly different overtones of the sanskrit original and a comparative study using more than one of these is reward-ing. A comparison of four different translations, two by Charles Johnson, one by Chatterji and another by Prab-havananda and Isherwood, in many ways the most western-ised, brings out the following description of the four-fold mental instrument or interior organ of perception of man, which may be compared with the four elements in the analysis made by Dr. Soal. Thus the first element of the interior organ of consciousness, the non-spatial mind, has the function of gathering together and separating impulses, of considering the various aspects of an object, of postulating and doubting. The second element called variously intelligence, intellect, soul or buddhi by the various translators, is surely Dr. Soal's 'non-material soul or self which is capable of types of conscious experience'. Its function is to reach a judgement regarding what is perceived, or to determine the real nature of an object. As it has the quality of true judgement, it has the character of certainty as to the nature of things. So according to the commentators it has the character of an immediate realisation and perception of that which exists.

The third element of the human inner organ of perception is the 'I' focus or ego sense, given variously as the personal sense or ahankara, self-assertion, the ego. The function of this is to evoke self-consciousness, which results when the mental organ identifies itself with the body. Such identification occurs through the brain mechanism. There thus arises the thought of 'I' through the attribution of self-hood which leads to egoism and self-assertion. So in this combined description of the four commentaries one has a picture very close to Dr. Soal's description of an ego-focus associated with the brain and normal consciousness experiencing 'such types of thought and feeling as are useful for its ordinary terrestrial existence'.

Finally, there is the function of imagination or 'image building faculty'. This is said to be the faculty of holding consciousness steady on its object and drawing together material in the form of mental images which are full of emotional content. The tendency is to 'draw in that which is pleasing' and can hold the interest. These imagination-created images are the thoughts, sensations and feelings which are the mental states of experience of Dr. Soal's analysis.

Mind is the inner organ

So whether approached from within by the eastern metaphysical insight or from without by an attempt to deduce an hypothesis to explain scientific observations, it would appear that man's mind is an inner organ, or instrument, of perception with a focus of 'I-ness' associated with the brain. It has the capacity of throwing up a three-dimensional field of imagined images, thoughts and feelings, themselves not spatial in a physical sense, but related to space by some method of direct correlation. They appear in a mental field which is not the property of any one observer, but can only be termed a generalised mental field. Within this generalised field there is focused the human intelligence or reason, that capacity which enables man to make distinctions, assess, weigh and judge values by direct perception. This field has also focused within it the even more significant quality which we call buddhi, that quality of life and light and intuitive insight with its immediacy of direct awareness and apprehension. These two, intelligence and buddhi, make up the 'non-material self or soul capable of varied types of conscious experience'.

In the above study it has been shown that the western scientific method of experiment and analysis has come into the field of the eastern metaphysical insights as to the nature of mind. There is abundant evidence that further exploration in this manner would form a fruitful field of research.

There is plenty of material for such a study which, combining the best of western and eastern methods, should enable us to formulate a new metaphysic which would be acceptable to advancing scientific knowledge.

★

Note. It is significant that since the above was written, further trends in this direction have occurred. An interesting book by Dr. Sarasvati Chennakesavah, *The Concept of Mind in Indian Philosophy*, presents the eastern concept of mind to western readers, and indicates the importance of the Indian views to modern psychology, while a series of articles on spiritualism in the *Sunday Times*, 7th August 1960 concluded with suggestions concerning the nature of mind, very similar to those presented here as providing the key to spiritualistic and other psychic phenomena.

Here is a field where students have much to contribute.

ADDENDA

Extracts from the various translations of

'*The Crest Jewel of Wisdom*' (1)

THE SUBTILE BODY

Johnson [1st Edn (vv. 95/96)] (2)

Its interior powers are called mind (Manas), intelligence (Buddhi), the personal sense (Ahankara), and imagination

(Chitta), with their activities. The function of mind is the gathering together and separating of impulses; the function of intelligence is to reach a judgement regarding what is experienced; the function of the personal sense is the thought of 'I' through the attribution of self-hood; the function of imagination is to hold the consciousness steady on its object.

Chatterji (vv. 95/96) (3)

The manas, buddhi, ahankara and chitta with their functions, are called the internal instruments. Manas is so called by reason of its postulating and doubting, buddhi by reason of its property of arriving at a fixed judgement about objects, ahankara arises from egotism, and chitta is so called on account of its property of concentrating the mind on its own interest.

Johnson [2nd Edn (p. 20)] (4)

Then the inward activity, mind, soul, self-assertion, imagination, with their proper powers; mind ever intending and doubting; soul, with its character of uncertainty as to things; self-assertion, that falsely attributes the notion of 'I'; imagination, with its power of gathering itself together and directing itself to its object.

Prabhavananda & Isherwood (p. 55) (5)

The mental organ consists of mind, intellect, ego and the emotional nature. These are distinguished by their different functions. The function of mind is to consider the various aspects of an object. The function of the intellect is to determine the real nature of an object. Ego is the self-consciousness which arises when the mental organ identifies itself with the body. The tendency of the emotional nature is to draw to that which is pleasing.

THE MIND-FORMED VESTURE

Johnson [1st Edn (v. 170)]

The mind-formed vesture is formed of the powers of perception and the mind; it is the cause of the distinction between the notions of 'mine' and 'I'; it is active in making a distinction of names and numbers; as more potent it pervades and dominates the former vesture (body).

Johnson [2nd Edn (v. 167)]

Same as 1st Edn.

Chatterji (169)

The organs of sensation together with the manas form the mano-maya sheath which is the cause of the differentiation between 'I' and 'mine'. It is the result of ignorance; it fills the former sheath and it manifests its great power by distinguishing objects by names, etc.

Prabhavananda & Isherwood (p. 70)

The mind together with organs of perception forms the mental covering. It causes the sense of 'I' and 'mine'. It also causes us to discern objects. It is endowed with the powers and faculty of differentiating objects by giving them various names. It is manifest, enveloping the vital covering.

THE INTERIOR ORGANS

A.	B.	C.	D.
JOHNSON (I)	JOHNSON (II)	CHATTERJI	PRABHAVANANDA & ISHERWOOD
Interior Powers	*Inward Activity*	*Internal Instruments*	*Mental Organ*
1. Mind (Manas)	Mind	The Manas	Mind
2. Intelligence (Buddhi)	Soul	Buddhi	Intellect
3. The Personal Sense	Self-Assertion	Ahankara	Ego
4. Imagination (Chitta)	Imagination	Chitta	Emotional nature

INNER POWERS

1. *Mind*

   A. The function of mind is the gathering together and separating of impulses.
   B. Mind ever intending and doubting.
   C. Manas is so called by reason of its postulating and doubting.
   D. The function of mind is to consider the various aspects of an object.

2. *Intelligence*

   A. The function of intelligence is to reach a judgement regarding what is perceived.
   B. Soul with its character of certainty as to things.

    C. Buddhi by reason of its property at arriving at a fixed
       judgement about objects.

    D. The function of the Intellect is to determine the real
       nature of an object.

OUTER POWERS

3. *The personal sense*

    A. The function of the personal sense in the thought of
       'I' through the attribution of self-hood.

    B. Self-assertion that falsely attributes the notion of 'I'.

    C. Ahankara arises from egotism.

    D. Ego is the self-consciousness which arises when the
       mental organ identifies itself with body.

4. *Imagination*

    A. The function of imagination is to hold the conscious-
       ness steady on its object.

    B. Imagination with its power of gathering together and
       directing itself towards its object.

    C. Chitta is so called on account of the property of
       concentrating the mind on one's own interest.

    D. The tendency of the emotional nature is to draw in to
       that which is pleasing.

References

1. Shankara Acharya, *The Crest Jewel of Wisdom* (Vivekachudamani).

2. Johnson, Charles (1st Edn, vv. 95, 96; p. 16), The
   Quarterly Book Department, New York, 1925.

3. Chatterji, Mohini H. (vv. 95, 96; pp. 32, 33), The Theosophical Publishing House, Adyar, Madras, India, 1932.
4. Johnson, Charles (2nd Edn, p. 20), The Theosophical University Press, Corina, California, 1946.
5. Prabhavananda & Isherwood (p. 55).
6. F. S. C. Northrop, *The Meeting of East and West*, Macmillan, 1960.

Five senses

Many animals, birds, fish and insects exhibit strange skills that seem to defy explanation in terms of the five senses we know. Some of them can tell the time even in a darkened room, others can migrate through thousands of miles of sea or air to a place they knew before. Are these and other feats accomplished by sight, hearing, scent and so on—senses like ours but much keener—or are the creatures 'psychic', i.e. able to perceive in ways unknown to most of us? Has the tracker dog such an acute sense of smell—or does he psychometrise?

A paper in *Nature* reports what appears to be a hitherto unknown new sense in rats. Convincing evidence is provided that rats can detect X-rays, even at the rather feeble level of 0·05 roentgens/sec. This is not done through any indirect visual effect because blind rats are just as competent as normal animals (1).

The writer has never been conscious of X-rays applied diagnostically to at least five parts of his anatomy. It is true that in modern practice the rest of the body is carefully screened, so that the target sense organ, wherever it might be, may have escaped exposure. However it must surely get exposed sometime, yet patients do not claim to detect X-rays. So it does seem that rats have at least one extra sense; it is hard to believe that they have any occasion to detect such radiation so presumably it must normally serve some other purpose.

On the other hand we may ourselves have some unsuspected abilities. A man who worked for a certain Atomic Energy Authority declared that he could 'feel' penetrating beta rays, as emitted by radio-active phosphorus for example. He was not submitted to any tests and the claim might be dismissed as imagination, except that this man was a sceptical scientist, used to making accurate observation. The writer has not himself been conscious of any sensation from penetrating beta or gamma radiation from radio-isotopes.

The same issue of *Nature* that reported the rat experiments, also covered the surprising, though less convincingly demonstrated, claim that we can under favourable circumstances detect cosmic rays, namely individual pi-mesons. This involves no new sense: it was calculated that these particles had sufficient energy to cause visible fluorescence in the lens of the eye, so that a pale blue disc of light was the anticipated sensation. In practice several observers reported a tiny 'prick' of light corresponding with a pi-meson entering one eye (via a detecting counter). This must have been a very tedious experiment for the observer, because the rate of incidence was only about one a minute. Some events were missed and these were false positives, but statistical analyses showed correct responses significantly above chance expectation (2).

Another curious faculty that is well established is the ability to 'hear' the pulsed high-frequency radio waves used for radar, when close to the transmitter. The normal auditory mechanism is not involved, for these sounds can be perceived by deaf people. They proved difficult to match against synthetic audio-frequency sounds, the closest approximation being to the generator ripple of the transmitter. Screening experiments showed the perception occurs only over an area of a few square inches around the temples, and it seems possible that the effect is directly upon the brain. With a hidden revolving antenna, subjects could detect the beam the instant it impinged upon them, but were quite unable to locate its source in space; the sound always appeared to come from just behind the head (3).

References

1. J. Garcia *et al.*, *Nature*, 1962 Vol. 196, 1014.
2. F. J. D'Arcy and N. A. Porter, *ibid.*, p. 1013.
3. Allan H. Frey, *J. Applied Physiology*, July 1962, *17*, 689.

The difference between spiritual and psychic perception

Very few people have as yet consciously realised the distinction between psyche, soul or mind, and spirit, yet the difference is very important, especially when it comes to matters of perception. For on true perception depends the truth or otherwise of our knowledge of the world in which we live.

The psyche lies between the physical and the spiritual worlds. It is the 'web' between spirit and matter. So the psyche partakes of the qualities of both these worlds. Within the psyche is the focus of conscious and willed living we call 'I'. The movement of evolving consciousness —that is, of 'I' in each one of us—is from the physical towards the spiritual, and as it rises, so does the quality of that consciousness change. The essence of physical consciousness is the acquisition of clarity of focus on a particular subject. This is achieved by a process of exclusion of apparently irrelevant material. The quality of spiritual consciousness, on the other hand, is inclusiveness. Things are there seen in context and relationship, not in isolation from the world in which they exist. Paradoxically, this does not, as it would in the case of physical consciousness, blur the capacity of the perception of detail. It includes the most minute detail in the whole picture of the subject under investigation. This is logical if we recall that the relationship or context of any object consists first of its position vis-à-vis the smaller items of which it is composed: for example, the

F

body to its cells. Then there is the relationship of the particular object to the greater unit in which it belongs: the earth to the solar system, the human being to mankind, and so on, in all directions. It is only when all these are included that a full and true picture of anything is obtained. The total picture is what we shall call the 'spiritual' one; it would obviously be incomplete without the clearly defined and focused quality which results from developed physical perceptivity. It would otherwise be nebulous and unclear.

Thus, while 'spiritual' perception gives a clear and total and true image of an object or a situation, physical perception must of necessity give only one which is partial, hence 'illusory'. Spiritual perception, the only true one, requires for its proper functioning, to include the qualities of clear physical perception as well as its own peculiar 'total' quality.

The direct perception of the psychic level lies somewhere between these two extremes. It derives primarily from the physical world, indeed represents an extension and expansion of that level of perception. It is truly 'extra-sensory' perception, in that it has the quality of physical sensation without, however, depending on the physical sense organs for its occurrence. It is the kind of psychism which belongs to the animal kingdom. It seems there to be almost entirely unconscious, provoking action on an instinctive pattern and, indeed, it is linked with instinct at a preconscious level. Only as human individuality develops does it become conscious and, at the same time, begins to acquire something of a spiritual quality. This latter occurs as the super-personal, or true self begins to operate and to infuse the ordinary mind with its own energies, and so, in transforming this mind, transforms also the quality of its perceptivity. In other words, '*psychism*' *only becomes spiritual in any degree when the mind of the individual also becomes spiritualised.*

It may be said in parenthesis that some people—Freud being one of them—suggest that E.S.P. or psychic perceptivity is a precursor to physical sense perception: that, as physical sense organs evolved, the more archaic root of perceptivity became vestigial, and its working was taken over by the physical organs. There may be some element of truth in this if we accept the idea that the present entities existed before there were physical bodies in which they could incarnate. But this is a different matter from the idea put forward above, which is supposed to rest on the evolution of physically incarnated life out of the mineral and through the other kingdoms to man. Indeed, the very simplest animal, the amoeba, certainly has no sense organs akin to eye or ear; but it is itself, as a whole, a sense organ, responsive to physical stimuli arising outside itself. Evolutionary study shows that what we have now evolves from the primitive sensitivity of the amoeba without needing to have recourse to 'psychic' or mental perceptivity coming from a mind more developed than the organism through which it works. (True, there may well be such a mind: the devic or divine mind. But it lies behind and removed from whatever mind the simple animal may have of its own, even if it directs that animal's evolution by remote control. This however, has little to do with the evolution of perceptivity by the animal itself.)

Whatever E.S.P. there may be in the early stages is not one of conscious perceptivity as ordinarily understood, but an unconscious, or truly subconscious stimulus to certain instinctive action-patterns. When we come to *conscious* perception at the psychic level, we enter a whole new range of events which, developing as conscious percepts, are couched in terms of the highly differentiated realm of physical awareness.

Why is psychic perceptivity often confused?

Why then, it may be asked, is psychic perceptivity so often diffuse and confused? The answer may be that it is still, for the average human being, at the stage where the animal had only primitive physical sense organs, and hence perceived only in a simple and undifferentiated manner. The psychic 'organs', *the chakras*, or mental equivalents of the physical sense organs, are still rudimentary. It requires the infusion of new forces, those associated with self-identity, through the mind to carry them further than the negative or passive form of E.S.P. which is still more the rule than the exception.

Another confusing factor is that of language. It is derived from what we know of the physical world. In the first instance language may be looked upon as a means of communication with others, but it also serves as a means to clarification of ideas within one's own mind. It limits the expression of psychic knowledge, which often represents situations or objects for which there is no physical counterpart. An example of this is when a clairvoyant speaks of colours as green or blue, knowing all along that this is a crude and even misleading description of what he actually sees; just as the attempt to relate size to an entirely different scale of space, or of duration to physical clock time.

These things apply to psychic perception considered as an extension from the physical level 'upward', growing out of the ground, as it were. Spiritual perception, on the other hand, is something of a still more different order, where expression and description becomes even more difficult.

There are no words for spiritual percepts except through paradox and seeming contradiction. It is a growth of perception, as it were 'downward' from the world of no-form towards that of form, and all forms are too small for it. Its whole quality is different.

When we come to practical issues, it has to be realised that the average man habitually dwells on a level nearer the physical pole of himself than the spiritual, so that his normal perceptive level is more like the physical than the spiritual. It is only at peak moments that he experiences the higher order of perceptivity which we have called spiritual. Many have attempted to tell others of what is seen in such moments, but the only reliable way is through silent communion which requires no verbalisation. With it comes, as a rule, a sense of infinitude, of profound unity with every creature, and perhaps particularly with the one one loves. It can also occur as a break-through in moments of great stress, pain or fear; and if sought through meditation and the real form of prayer. The ordinary person touches such experience momentarily, but the purpose behind all religious and spiritual training is to achieve such a state, if not permanently, at least, at will.

There is another and most important aspect of spiritual perception which we often fail to realise. We, have, so far, emphasised in this paper the contrast between physical and spiritual perception, saying that they were literally 'poles apart'. In fact, of course, there is no such arbitrary division except in theory or at the very 'ends' of the total range. There is no pure black or pure white in nature. In the same way perceptivity is always mixed. It is difficult to say with any degree of accuracy, 'This is spiritual, that is physical or psychic.'

Spiritual and physical contrasts

It will help if we remember what has been said about the completeness of the contrast between physical and spiritual because the latter is characterised by its all-inclusiveness, embodying in itself all the qualities of all forms of perception including the physical. For we can then see that there may be a high degree of spiritual perception when a physical object is being observed through the physical senses. Ordinarily it may be suggested, the only spiritual element in such a perception would be conscious awareness of it, indicating a sense of 'Me' observing 'It'. But there are times when a trivial incident takes on a new quality and becomes illumined with transcendentalism. On the feeling side there is a sense of expansion or joy; on the intellectual, however, it brings a Gestalt of new meaning and significance. Leaving aside the matter of the state of inner preparedness of the percipient, the effect is one of discovery. Whether the story of Newton's apple is historical or not, it exemplifies a moment of spiritual insight, attached to a minor physical event: he suddenly saw the principle of gravity. Einstein similarly had such a moment when he saw the basic principle of relativity. Darwin must have had a sudden integrative moment when he saw that of evolution.

It is thus the creative background to any experience which shows the infusion into the everyday world of spiritual perceptivity, supplementing and transforming physical perceptions, or one's thought patterns or one's feeling attitudes. Moreover, such new insight or discovery may work within a limited field only. It is not only the one who experiences 'cosmic consciousness' or some other most profound and self-transmuting vision who experiences spiritual perception, but each person who finds a new view of some physical object or situation. There is thus no need to hunt far afield and demand some personality-shattering event, in order to experience the perception of spirit. It is much more a matter of feeling out for a certain quality in everyday life—feeling for, but not actively reaching out and trying to command it. On the contrary, a relaxed, passive-alert state of mind is at the back of it, an openness of feeling, and hence contentment. It may then be found at any moment and in connection with the most humdrum circumstances, if one's inner eyes are open.

It is clear how different such a thing is from ordinary psychic perception. Generally speaking most of this tends to be of a very mundane order, often diffuse and vague, and possibly factually inaccurate. As with physical perceptivity, it achieves real value when the spiritual element comes into play, though this does not of necessity eliminate error and distortion in any direct manner. It may act only by making the percipient aware of the fact that he is distorting things, allowing his thoughts and feelings, his preconceptions and mental rigidities to intervene between himself and the thing as it really is. For the 'psychic' of necessity sees things through his own mind, always more or less coloured and, distorted as by a lens. He is in a similar position to the observer of physical events, since it is well established that the actual organs of sight, hearing, etc., vary between individuals both in quality and range, and so present to each one of us only a highly personalised and 'unreal' picture of the world.

Spiritual aspect essential for true perception

This personal world-image can be corrected and aligned
with reality only as the spiritual aspect of the individual
comes increasingly into play. That is why every true
teacher of matters spiritual deprecates the attempt to develop
'siddhis' or psychic powers as an end in itself. The result can
only be confusion through the extension of physical sensations into a world of plastic, indefinite forms; moreover the
mind actively or passively full of images is itself an imperfect
organ of perception. Further, this mind impinges on the
psychic objects and changes them according to what it
feels or thinks about them: until it has acquired a high degree
of detachment and objectivity (*viveka* and *vairagya*) it cannot
look at a thing without at the same time acting upon and
changing it. Spiritual vision or insight in its fullest form is
direct, immediate, unconditioned, cognition. It depends in
no way on clairvoyance or other forms of E.S.P., but on the
contrary true and accurate E.S.P. does depend on spiritual
insight; hence the futility of trying to develop clairvoyance
or other forms of psychic perceptivity by artificial methods
like hypnosis, 'sitting for development', various forms of
yoga other than the true Raja Yoga, and so on. Unless an
individual is already highly trained, as we shall try to
explain later, only a primitive unfocused kind of perceptivity can result. This is often demonstrated in groups
and seances, where passive forms of mediumship are
the order of the day. There is only one royal road to true
perceptivity, which is through the pursuit of Truth or
spiritual insight, by whatever means are most suited to the
individual.

A good many people try 'astral projection', strenuous

breathing exercises, and so on, and if they do not possess the necessary spiritual and psychological stability, will often find themselves in a morass of confusion, or even disaster. This may seem too dogmatic and categorical a condemnation of various common practices, and indeed it needs to be qualified. For as we have mentioned, a flash of spiritual insight may occasionally occur anywhere and at any time.

Similarly, when people use the highly dangerous psychedelic drugs, if they are inwardly prepared, they may come back from the experience changed by having seen something infinitely precious to them. They may, on the other hand, find themselves looking into a pit of desolation, a private hell existing in their own unconscious mind. Aldous Huxley, in the first flush of enthusiasm for mescalin, wrote a fascinating account of what he saw, one which rings true; but he later added to his essay on 'The Doors of Perception' a second and corrective one which he entitled 'Heaven and Hell'.

There is need to account for such things, and for the differences between individuals. This can only be done if we are prepared to consider the still unscientific hypothesis of the etheric or vital field. The effect of drugs in general is said to alter this field. The psychedelic or hallucinogenic drugs, more than any others, do so at the perceptive level (though hashish, alcohol, and many others have at least some effect there too). This would take place at the level of the middle of the field, thinning—and in some cases destroying, with disastrous results—the screening or censoring function of this layer, and so opening up the psychic world to the subject. What he then sees, and what 'layers' of the psychic world he contacts depends on his own inner stage. If he is spiritually awake, he seems likely to go 'higher' or 'deeper' than one who is not, and who lacks true sensitivity and is personally self-centred and self-interested.

These drugs are dangerous if given to unsuitable people, because latent instability may get out of control—as the wiser experimenters are at last realising. They become victims of their unconscious, which invades the conscious field and remains there, and the result is insanity. In other words a psychosis which might have remained latent becomes active and destructive. There are instances, however, where the drugs, by artificially thinning the veil, seem to work by allowing consciousness to bypass the over-trained intellect of the subject so that for the first time he experiences what lies behind that intellect. What he finds is often something 'he has known all the time', but refused to consider because it would have upset the logical structure of his mind. It should be added, too, that some people are practically unaffected by a dose of drug. Their etheric field is too tough to respond, just as some people are virtually immune to some forms of natural poisons.

Why some people are psychic from birth

Another question which must arise in connection with this subject is why some people are born naturally 'psychic', whether in general sensitivity or in some particular manner. Undoubtedly physical heredity plays a part in this, giving a certain foundation to the general etheric field of a child; but psychological conditioning may play as large a part, in that a child brought up from birth to a materialistic viewpoint is less likely to retain the natural sensitivity most children have, and which would be fostered in a family where the less rational and the intangible are taken as part of life. Then there arises the question of previous training, in older times. This clearly involves the matter of reincarnation of individuals as 'themselves', bringing with them at least some measure of the skills in which they were trained, probably in ancient mystery schools.

This at once raises the further question as to whether these schools still exist, perhaps even among those which advertise training—for a consideration—in 'astral projection', growth of power over others and similar things. One needs to realise that the true Mysteries have always existed and probably still do. But they operate in total secrecy, admitting to their ranks only those who are seeking Truth and nothing more mundane. Whether training in clairvoyance or other forms of E.S.P. is still given by a genuine 'Master' is dubious, in view of the very different conditions existing in the world today. It is no longer easy, if it is possible at all, to take an aspirant out of the world into a quiet community where he can be relieved of the chores of everyday life, secluded both physically and psychically (the latter especially), from a world where turmoil and haste and strife penetrates everywhere with hurricane force. Further, the mental fabric of mankind as a whole has changed, become crisp and tough by the demands of a scientific age which affects even the unscientific and untrained. There is perhaps much more than fantasy in Joan Grant's *Winged Pharaoh*: but it refers to a remote past in the history of mankind.

If, however, a person has had training and has learned clairvoyance with reasonable accuracy and steady focus, he may well be born today with this still active. It may, however, show only at a later stage of life, perhaps concurrently with some form of spiritual training. Or it may spring into evidence as a result of trauma. In general, it seems that a latent capacity comes out, rather than a new development out of nothing.

E.S.P., however, is clearly not dying out. On the contrary, it seems to be becoming more prominent, particularly among certain people. It is important, however, to see it for what it is, and particularly, not to set out to develop it in ways which can only lead to its regressive forms. It should be *beyond* the scientific attitude of mind, not a retreat from it, but an addition to true science, in its search for more and clearer knowledge, and hence a means of probing something of the deeper aspects of reality behind scientifically observed facts.

From a larger point of view, it is not the development of the psychic levels of the perceptive function which matters, but a search for an inward revelation of Truth, unique in each individual. If he is seeking this, it is inevitable that, eventually, the whole range of perceptivity must be his. His 'psychism', however, will develop—or redevelop— from the spiritual towards the physical levels, thus avoiding the pitfalls which lie in wait for the one who begins at the primitive instinctive level and tries to work in the opposite direction. Such can only become confused since spiritual insight is not sufficient in him to give light. No wonder that H. P. Blavatsky speaks of the danger and illusion of the 'middle realm', prematurely entered by one insufficiently trained and disciplined. To be safe, we need to clarify our minds both as to what is truly spiritual and what is psychic, what represents the bliss of the top 'octave' of feeling we call Buddhi and what is only emotional and Kamic, what is a true image and what is the product of more or less wishful thinking and ideation. This will also help us to discriminate between methods of self-training which are beneficial and those which are either useless, dangerous, or misleading in the quest for Truth.

Etheric vision and radiation

Practical investigations into etheric vision

In the investigation of subtle bodies and energy fields it may be that the 'other worlds'—which certainly exist—are the results of other types of consciousness, like dreaming, and that it is not sensible to speak of them as 'interpenetrating' the physical world, since they have no *spatial* relationship to the physical world.

The obvious level at which to start this investigation is the so-called etheric level, because traditional theosophical theory states that the etheric material is still physical, and therefore objective, in the sense that tables and chairs are objective. Also, one of several classical theories of etheric vision ('X-ray eyes') describes the 'etheric retina', said to be the subtle organ of vision involved, as situated a little behind the retina of the eye. This implies the use of light—perhaps in the normally invisible range—in clairvoyant observation of the etheric.

If the objectivity of the etheric plane could be established, that is, if its existence in physical space apart from the consciousness of the psychic could be shown, then in principle the possibility of its instrumental detection is immediately opened up. In particular, etheric material might be photographed, provided the right kind of light and the right photographic emulsion were used. Classical theory states that we all possess an 'etheric double' which interpenetrates the dense physical body, duplicating every cell, and which carries the 'life forces'. In particular, the appearance of disease in the physical body is said to be the result of disease in the etheric. If that is true, then photography of the etheric double would be of great value in medical diagnosis. In fact, treatment of the etheric double might prevent incipient disease appearing in the physical body at all. Many readers will be aware that radionic practitioners claim to treat the etheric double and claim that radionic diagnoses are of diseases in this subtler body—often discovered before they become overt at all. This was one of the major points brought out in the High Court case of 1960 in which Mr. G. W. de la Warr defended his radionic practices. 'Magnetic healers' also claim to treat the etheric body, removing undesirable etheric material by 'will power' and replacing it with fresh vitalised material of their own.

Regarding modern evidence that etheric material really exists, a number of books have been written in recent years describing the results of what is claimed to be etheric vision. It is used frequently in medical diagnosis and such diagnoses would appear often to be correct (though the writers on this subject seem singularly modest when one examines their reports for scientific evidence). Some remarks appear below on this matter of medical diagnosis.

Other modern evidence which may be relevant concerns ectoplasm. In materialisation seances clairvoyants sometimes describe a form invisible to non-psychic observers, and state that the form is densifying. In a short time the described form is visible to all present. There seems to be a difference only of degree and not of principle between this clairvoyance and ordinary sight. The classic work by Dr. F. Osty using infra-red light is perhaps pertinent. (The 1933 F. W. H. Myers lecture of the Soc. for Psychical Research.) Perhaps all this and similar material can now be collated, and new work done to give some scientific certainty regarding the

G

existence of etheric matter. If the classical theory is true—
that ectoplasm is temporarily densified material from the
medium's etheric double (perhaps with additional components)—then, *ipso facto*, etheric material exists.

Fundamental experiments

The experiments described below were therefore intended
to find out whether etheric material existed which was
objective to a psychic with the appropriate vision. If the
existence of the material were established it was intended to
arrange for some of it to be present in a known region of
space and to study the effects of various wavelengths of
light and of filters on the psychic's etheric vision with a view
to determining the best light to use in attempts at photography.

It may be remarked here that red light is usually used in
seances employing ectoplasm because it is less 'energetic'
than light of shorter wavelengths and has a less destructive
effect on the material. On the other hand, red light is very
penetrating and one might imagine that light of a shorter
wavelength, perhaps ultra-violet, would be more likely to
be reflected from etheric material and therefore enable it to
be photographed, or to cast a shadow on a photographic
plate.

The assistance was first obtained of a psychic who worked
regularly with a leading Spiritualist organisation. The
major experiment carried out was as follows.

It is believed by many people that when the fingers of the
two hands are pressed together and then withdrawn slightly,
streams of greyish mist are to be seen (if the lighting and
background are appropriate) which appear to join opposing
fingers. These streams are said to be of etheric material (part

of the etheric double) and affected by the will. If one 'wills' to make the flow stronger then it behaves appropriately. Sometimes little points of light are described as appearing at the tips of the fingers. The writer has many times received descriptions of this phenomenon put forward as evidence for the existence of the etheric body.

The writer conducted his experiment with the Spiritualist medium (who shall be called S.M.) in the following way. He asked S.M. to place the tips of his fingers together and then withdraw them slightly, enquiring whether he could observe the traditional streams of material. S.M. replied that he could see them very clearly. A little experimentation showed that the clearest vision was obtained in a good light with the psychic's back to the window.

S.M. described the streams as bluish grey and slightly self-luminous (and he felt as though his fingers were being drawn together). He stated that all his fingers and both hands were surrounded by a glow, pulsating like a heart beat. A small ball of glowing greyish-blue material appeared, he said, between his middle finger-tips. Slowly, as his vision improved, he observed three colours in the streams, blue, grey (in the centre) and reddish (outside). He could observe a similar effect when the writer's fingers were arranged in the same way, in fact the reddish glow 'streamed out from the region around each hand, met in the middle, and poured upwards like a candle flame'. When the writer informed S.M. that he was 'willing' the stream to increase (and did so) it became 'very powerful' to S.M.'s vision.

A cardboard box was now brought into use, containing slits so arranged in conjunction with a cardboard mask that the writer's hands could be placed within the box and his

two sets of fingers placed the same distance apart as before.
The hands and fingers were completely hidden from S.M.'s
view, only the space between them being visible to him
through the slit. The box was examined and its purpose in
screening the fingers, while leaving the space between them
clearly visible as before, was explained to S.M.

The writer now placed his hands in the box and arranged
his fingers at each side of the slit through which S.M. was
looking. The slit was immediately filled, to S.M.'s vision,
with the red glow described above. The fingers were now
taken away from the slit (S.M. being fully informed) and
the red glow died away in about two minutes. When the
fingers were replaced (keeping S.M. informed) the red glow
reappeared. When the writer's two hands were placed flat
on the bottom of the box a very much paler glow was
visible to S.M. through the slit. S.M. stated that he certainly
thought he could tell when the writer's fingers were on each
side of the slit, and when they were removed and placed on
the bottom of the box.

The writer then placed his hands flat on the bottom of the
box and asked S.M. to tell him when they were placed at
the slit and when they were removed. S.M. was informed
that the intervals would be quite long (in view of the
apparent two-minute dying away time of the red glow).
S.M. then made remarks in the following manner: 'Now
they are there' . . . 'Now they are not' . . . 'Now there' . . .
'Not' . . . 'Yes' . . . 'No' . . . etc.

During this part of the experiment the writer at no time
moved his hands from the bottom of the box. S.M.'s
remarks bore no relation whatever to the position of the
writer's fingers. In fact they were at the end surreptitiously
removed from the box altogether and folded on his lap.

S.M. continued to describe the colours, which appeared and disappeared (to his psychic vision) at the slit.

The result of this experiment was quite unequivocal. There was no correlation whatever between the psychic vision and the position of the fingers, and presumably of any etheric material between them. The psychic's 'vision' was produced by what is sometimes called 'unconscious dramatisation'–a psychological phenomenon–and bore no relationship to 'reality' by way of the position of the fingers.

It is perhaps not without significance that following the above experiment—and the psychic was *not* told the results and assumed that he 'saw' correctly all the time—another experiment was carried out. The fingers were placed a little apart as before (in full view) and pairs of thin plates of various materials were placed closely against the fingers of each hand. The 'flow of etheric material' would therefore have to pass through two parallel plates on its way from one finger to the other on the opposite hand. Plates of brass, steel, cardboard and Perspex were used. Distinct differences in the intensity of the glow between the opposite fingers were observed by S.M. when the plates were changed to a different material, and it would be possible to make up a list of materials in order of 'inhibiting etheric flow power'. The writer suggests that there would be little point in doing any such thing. This is described here in order to illustrate the way in which some experimenters of the past have been led sadly astray by experiments which have assumed too much, i.e. which have not been sufficiently fundamental. There is no point in studying objective etheric vision until one has first established that it exists. If a psychic cannot tell whether etheric material (which he assumes to exist) is present or not there is no point in going into detail.

Similar experiments, which will not be described here in detail for obvious reasons, were made with an electro-magnet. When the current was switched on—and an electromagnetic field therefore existed in its airgap—S.M. could see a 'red Glow' in the gap. When the current was switched off (and he knew) the red glow slowly died away. The experiment involved switching the current on and off at intervals without S.M.'s knowledge, and asking him to state by observation of the airgap whether the field existed or not. Again, no correlation whatever existed between his psychic observations of the gap and the state of the current.

The psychic S.M. was not told at any time the results of the experiments, but full notes were taken by the writer.

The above reports only two experiments with one psychic, and it is obvious that the psychic tested did not have the particular kind of objective clairvoyance for which we were looking, though *he was convinced he had*, in all sincerity.

Such experiments do not prove that etheric vision does not exist in some persons, but demonstrates the absolute necessity of not accepting the statements of a clairvoyant without first taking most stringent precautions against self-deception, and even if this is done with apparent success, the experiment in addition must be so arranged as to eliminate the possibility of telepathic communication.

ADDENDUM

A NOTE ON KILNER GOGGLES

There are available from more than one source so-called Kilner goggles which are supposed to give the wearer the ability to see the human 'aura'. A suggested explanation of how these work would appear to be relevant to the present reports of experimental work on etheric vision.

A member of the Science Group acquired a pair of Kilner goggles and measured their light transmission characteristics, i.e. the proportion of incident light which is transmitted through the goggles for a range of wavelengths covering the visible spectrum and beyond.

The results showed that the Kilner goggles tested transmit very little light over most of the visible spectrum, but they do transmit two small bands of visible light, one at the blue end and one at the red end of the spectrum. If one puts on the goggles and looks at an illuminated object through them, then the eyes will receive only these two bands of visible light. It would appear that if one focused the eyes so that a clear image was obtained on the retina for one of the bands, then the band of light at the other end of the spectrum would necessarily be slightly out of focus. A blurred image due to the latter would result, which would appear superimposed on the first image but projecting all round it as a haze. The latter would be the 'aura'. This theory might be verified, or disproved, if someone is found who can 'see the aura' through the goggles. The addition, in front of their eyes, of a filter to cut out the small band of visible light at one end of the spectrum would cause the 'aura' to disappear, if the theory is correct.

A similar explanation probably applies to the kind of Kilner screen which is used to 'sensitise' the eyes, the aura then being observed directly. In this case a bright light is observed through the screen for some time in the process of sensitising the eyes. If the screen is so constituted that only light in the middle of the visible spectrum is allowed through, then the eyes will become tired so far as this range of colours (or wavelengths) is concerned. If the illuminated object, which may be another person, is now observed, it will be seen by light at the two ends of the spectrum, to which the eyes will still be sensitive. A sharp and a blurred image may then be expected, and the pseudo 'aura' seen as before. It is not everyone who can use these Kilner devices to see the 'aura'. Presumably one needs the ability to focus one of the two bands of visible light, while 'ignoring' the other. The skill can be acquired with practice, sometimes!

There may be readers who know of cases where a person has used a Kilner device to look at the 'aura' of a patient and has correctly diagnosed the presence of disease by the dark patches on the 'etheric aura'. Psychics with etheric sight can sometimes do this without a Kilner device. The explanation may be as follows.

E.S.P., or 'psi faculty', exists. There is no reasonable doubt about that. Some psychics perhaps have the faculty of discovering what is wrong with a patient without using any of the normal means. How they know is a complete mystery, like the mechanism of telepathy. The desired information appears in the unconscious. The unconscious selects one of several possible ways of presenting it to the conscious mind. One way might be to produce a vision in a crystal. Another way might be to make blurred patches on a patient's badly focused image, i.e. 'dark areas on the aura'. If the psychic who has this experience has been brought up on a mental diet of classical theosophical books he will naturally interpret the experience given to him by the unconscious (the nature of which is unknown to him) in terms of 'etheric vision'. He will naturally assume that it is objective, i.e. that he is really looking at the patient's 'subtle body'. It could easily be that the true source of the information about the patient's inside came from the mind of the doctor in charge. How can the psychic tell?

It is emphasised once again that the above is only *one* explanation of what is sometimes a very useful faculty. However, it may often be the true explanation. We have not yet established the existence of the classical objective etheric vision.

In search of the etheric

It has often been said that concentrated radiations from the etheric double can be seen projecting from the finger-tips if they are viewed against a dark background, and that these radiations can be intensified if the fingers of the other hand are held opposite them with a short space between the finger-tips.

In an endeavour to repeat this experiment, fingers were examined against a dead black velvet background with a moderate light behind the observer, and a greyish mist was seen projecting beyond the tips of each finger.

On placing the corresponding fingers of the other hand opposite, leaving a gap of about $1\frac{1}{2}$ inches, the faint mist from each finger linked up with that of its fellow on the opposite hand to form a bridge in each case, and when one hand was raised or lowered in this position, the bridge of mist continued to link up with its fellow at an oblique angle.

Since it has been reported that some people can see the etheric more clearly after gazing through a blue glass at a bright light, the observer looked through a blue filter (Ilford 306) at some clouds for a minute or so, and then repeated the finger experiment. This confirmed the report, for the mist appeared to be slightly more intense than when examined without first using the blue filter.

During these experiments it had been noticed that when the fingers were moved up or down, not only was there a misty projection in line with the fingers, but also a slight misty trail, like very faint smoke, following behind the brightest part of the finger-nails as they moved up or down. As this did not fit in with anything the experimenter had read about the etheric, other tests were tried and it was found that when a finger was stationary, and the mist was standing straight out from the finger, the former could be made to turn upwards at an angle of forty-five degrees from the finger-tip by simply looking at the tip, and then along the path one wished the mist to go. This happened each time it was tried, whether up or down, and without using a finger on the opposite side to act as an intensifyer, so that it appeared as if an effort of will was deflecting the mist upwards or downwards without moving the finger or any other finger opposite.

Although these findings tended to confirm much of what had been read, it still did not explain the smoke-like trail that had been seen following the bright area on the finger-nail when the finger moved, suggesting that what one was really seeing was a demonstration of the persistence of vision when a moving object is seen against a contrasting background. But while this would explain the smoke trail behind the moving finger-nail, it did not explain the projection of apparent mist beyond the finger-tip when it was *stationary*. However, on further careful examination of what had been done when making these observations one realised that it was the movement of the eyes along the line of the finger and beyond the tip and back again, that was creating the illusion of a projecting mist. This could be made to travel along any visual path the eyes traced on the black velvet, provided they started from a bright object, or better still a bright spot (finger-nail) on that object. The mist would be intensified when holding another finger opposite, because, as one looked very rapidly from tip to tip, the second finger would provide an extra luminous spot for the eye to take back with it, along its visual path as it returned to the first finger-tip.

From further careful examinations of the forms the mist took in different experiments, one came to the conclusion that two phenomena were being experienced at the same time. One, the persistence of vision when the eye or object is moving, and two, the tired retina effect when one looks at an object, and then at a plain background and sees a subjective image of the object (with the light and shade reversed).

Finally, to make quite sure that this was the explanation of what had been seen, a screen with a gap in it was placed between the eyes and fingers so that the fingers could be seen through the gap, or withdrawn slightly to the side out of sight. The experiments were repeated, and when the finger-tips were visible, the mist effects already described were also visible, but when the fingers were withdrawn a little, while still being opposite one another, the mist gradually faded and did not return unless the fingers were once more made visible. It was also shown that the appearance of the mist was not dependent on the distance between the finger-tips, which varied from a quarter to two inches, nor on imagination, since the observer knew where his fingers were, even when they could not be seen, but was entirely dependent on the visibility of the fingers.

There remained the question of the blue filter, and after a number of tests with different colour screens, it appeared that looking through the blue filter (which excluded all red light), temporarily increased the sensitivity of the retina to red, so that when one looked at pink fingers, they appeared with greater intensity after using the screen than when using the eyes without it. The subjective images produced by the fingers were therefore also increased in intensity.

Finally, in order to exclude the possibility of any unknown vital radiations from a living hand, a number of inanimate objects such as wooden spatulas, and collar stiffeners were used instead of fingers, and all the experiments repeated. The results were exactly the same as before. When the objects were visible their 'auras' and apparent projections were visible, but when the objects were just out of sight, the misty images disappeared.

Although what at first sight seemed to be etheric vision proved to be only a normal phenomenon, it does not follow that there are no etheric radiations from finger-tips, or that a clairvoyant who sees such radiations is not seeing something which has objective reality.

It does however mean that hundreds of past experiments of this kind where the fingers were visible to the observer, have now been rendered invalid, and shows the absolute necessity of screening the fingers from the observer in all future experiments of a similar nature, whether the observer is a clairvoyant or not.

The human aura

For centuries religious art has shown forms of human aura which range from the single halo encircling a sanctified head to the general personal radiation depicted in the Mexican image of the Virgin of Guadalupe. Right up to the present day clairvoyants describe forms of auric colourings around a person which may be swiftly flowing, brilliant hues or dull grey mists which cling closely to the physical form. Since the possession of one or more auras is harmless, it might be considered not to matter very much whether the whole concept arose from a need for a symbol of spiritual enlightenment or if, indeed, there has always been some experiential basis; but what has made the verification of the aura a worthwhile quest is the implication its confirmed presence would have for theories about the total constitution of Man. If there is some human phenomenon of this kind that changes with predominant moods, for instance, then some highly personal energy source is responsible for it; this would need explaining and could well favour one theory and embarrass another.

Taking an overall view of the possibilities, a first basic division is that either the aura idea is purely subjective or symbolic and without any observational basis, or it has some external reality to be sensed whatever the process of perceiving may be. Failure to establish any experimental evidence for an objective aura phenomenon external to the perceiver will make the symbolic explanation more and more likely merely by default, for any positive indications away from symbolism must depend on what is brought to light by investigation. If, for instance, the aura arises within the 'observer' purely as a subconscious dramatisation of ideas about the person observed, then the 'observation' contains nothing objective concerning the aura beyond the presence of the observed to act as an incentive to dramatise. This purely internal, subjective activity would be a case of symbolic representation just as much as a more extrovert expression in art.

To pursue this matter, therefore, evidence must be sought on the assumption that it is there to be found in the realms of the physical, the psychic or the psychological. Three alternatives seem to present themselves here. Firstly, that some types of aura are radiations from a person's form, probably conforming to the known laws of energy emission such as in any part of the electro-magnetic spectrum. Secondly, that some physical state or phenomenon is being perceived through a parapsychological (or psychic) process within the percipient which is then portrayed to his own inner 'vision' as an aura. Or, thirdly, that some psychic phenomenon or psychological state is being sensed by a psychic process in the observer and, again, is being pictorially demonstrated to him ostensibly as normal vision.

Hypothesis—energy emission perceived by the eye

Only the first of these possibilities, the radiation concept, is largely within the realm of the natural sciences, the other two depending on less understood laws of the psyche. For this reason most of the recorded effort and speculation has been given first to searching within the context of illumination and optical phenomena where the laws are mostly known and experimental methods can follow established practice.

An aura found by these means will probably be intimately associated in essence and function with the physical organism.

It is theoretically possible, although very tedious, to examine and eliminate one by one all the forms of natural energy radiation by making receptive apparatus of the required sensitivity which would record the radiation if it were there. For example, any physical body at a temperature above absolute zero radiates some heat energy in the infra-red region of the electro-magnetic spectrum and there are normal techniques for recording this such as electronic crystal detectors, image converter tubes and infra-red photography. However, pictures showing the physical body differentiated by its slowly changing temperature gradients have not been accepted as representing any of the auras in question. Are there any other human radiations lying between radio waves and cosmic waves which might be more favourably interpreted?

Normal photography depends on light supplied by a source which is modified by reflection or transmission at the object, but it is still a radiation which finally reaches the observer. Can a person modify some kind of incident radiation so that it becomes visible to the physical eye as an aura? This line of thought must include the possibilities of fluorescence.

Incoming radiation, however, is only part of the perceiving process. A problem arises from the fact that the light energy arriving at a 'seeing' observer only gives what is known as 'sight' after passing through complicated electro-chemical processes in the eye-ball and optic nerve, followed by even less understood scanning and interpretative operations in the brain and its associated consciousness.

This was exemplified by experiments in which goggles ('Stratton's spectacles') were worn continuously to invert the images of the outside world on both retinas. After an uncomfortable period of readjustment, the wearer was again able to see images the right way up, drive a car, read and carry on all his usual activities. When the goggles were removed so that the normal optical arrangement was restored, an even more unpleasant period of nausea and dizziness occurred, but image perception was once more inverted so that he was conscious of the correct orientation.

Experiments can be carried out by clairvoyants which include this part of the perception process and check their overall consciousness directly against the electro-magnetic radiation hypothesis while they view the aura in their normal way. One method employs a series of colour filters so chosen that they form a clear-cut but continuous succession, each passing only a certain band of wave-lengths. As the aura is viewed through these, the theory would predict that if vision were stopped by some filters but was unhindered by others, then the wavelength involved could be isolated.

A more basic form of experiment is the use of randomising and automatic recording apparatus to check that vision of the aura is accurate and repeatable when all telepathic or other psychic means of obtaining the information have been eliminated. Only when this has been established for a particular psychic is the coloured filter experiment really meaningful.

Unfortunately, an indeterminacy often creeps into the practical conduct of these experiments due to the very nature of the human clairvoyant faculty and a good deal of work remains to be done before any firm conclusions can be drawn.

H

To confuse the issue further, the eye has its own independent response to incoming radiation; the lens has absorption
bands which allow only 10 to 15% transmission at a wavelength of 405 milli-microns (mμ) in the ultra-violet and only
0·1% at 365 mμ. These figures can vary over a 10:1 range
for individuals and ageing increases the wavelength at which
absorption starts. Children can usually see down to 300 mμ
at which level the other components of the eye start to
absorb as well. Adults who have had their lenses removed
can again see easily by light of 365 mμ which is darkness to
normal eyesight. This absorbing feature of the lens and
other eye components acts as a protection for the retina
which becomes irritated and inflamed by radiation below
310 mμ. Since clairvoyants do not especially complain of
retinitis, this might indicate that if the aura involved radiation in the ultra-violet, then it was above 310 mμ wavelength but below 430 mμ, or else everyone would see it.
Do the majority of successful clairvoyants who see the aura
have outstanding vision somewhere in the range 310–430
mμ?

An observation which might favour the radiation hypothesis and also indicates one part of the spectrum more than
another is that some clairvoyants report their viewing of the
aura to be by oblique vision and not by direct gaze. From
the structure of the eye the inference from this is that the
fovea is not used, but rather the surrounding areas of the
retina. Now, the central fovea is equipped mainly with
cone receptors which are used for colour discrimination and
vision in high luminance, while the surrounding retina has
mainly rods with their visual purple content which only
perceive the blue end of the spectrum and are responsible for
vision when the illumination is low. Deep-sea fish, bats,

owls and many other creatures with nocturnal habits possess only rod equipped retinas, whereas some diurnal animals like birds and lizards have only cones.

Although there are animals which do not conform to this general distinction, it is fair to deduce that if human vision of the aura is by the normal photochemical action of the rods, then the wavelengths concerned correspond to blue or ultra-violet rather than the visible or infra-red end of the spectrum.

A further peculiarity of the eye is that under ultra-violet radiation the lens will fluoresce and emit a continuous spectrum of its own up to 600 mμ with a maximum energy at about 425 mμ; this causes an out-of-focus bluish haze when it impinges on the retina. Not only the lens but also the retina can fluoresce with a greenish blue which will be superimposed on the true incoming ultra-violet to give a lavender-grey colour. Do the combined ultra-violet fluorescences of lens and retina, or either on its own, in any way explain the greyish aura around objects reported by some clairvoyants? Are there any other natural human radiations which could give rise to similar fluorescence and vision in an eye of the right characteristics? Tests could probably be devised to give indications.

A way of conditioning the physical eye was used in the classical work of Dr. Walter J. Kilner who also subscribed to the theory that the aura was an objective phenomenon of the person observed. In his book *The Human Atmosphere*, he described how the use of dicyanin screens sensitised the eyes to the aura in a cumulative and two-fold way. They shortened the focal-length of the eyes for white light, so that true focusing on the retina occurred more for the blue end of the spectrum and they also gave hyper-sensitivity to some unusual wavelengths with reduced response to other visible colours.

After sensitising with the screens, an aura was said to be plainly visible in dim light, but not in darkness. It was in two parts, an inner component two or three inches wide, close to the body outline and an outer aura fading to nothing, up to a foot or more from the body. In contrast to other more vivid and volatile forms described by other people, the aura colours he saw were usually blue, bluey-green, bluey-grey or grey; they were slow moving and kept roughly to the body shape. The size of the outer aura could usually be influenced by static-electricity charges, its colour could be altered by fumigating the skin with substances such as iodine, chlorine or bromine, and both size and shape changed with the state of health and physical development.

Screens of different colours like deep carmine, light carmine and pale blue were used for their differential effect on inner and outer aura visibilities, blue being generally best for observing the outer and red for the inner. Dr. Kilner believed that the wavelengths of the auras he observed were in the ultra-violet region, but an accepted interpretation of his findings has yet to be formulated; repetition of his experiments has also been scanty and inconclusive.

Any theory of the aura as an electro-magnetic radiation has to deal with the question of clothing and its effect, or lack of effect. Dr. Kilner viewed the aura phenomena of his patients with clothing removed but most clairvoyants do not require this, in which case the assumed radiation is not impeded by material. Considerable technical difficulties are encountered in suggesting how the energy could be electro-magnetic in these circumstances.

Concerning other influences around the body which

might effect an observer, an electro-static field exists around the human body and all living organisms. Studies by H. S. Burr and L. J. Ravitz in America showed that this very weak field could be measured by micro- and milli-volt meters and its variations correlated well with different emotional, mental and physical states. It was found possible to differentiate between the effects of hypnosis, sleep and drugs; nervous and mental abnormalities could be identified by their characteristic patterns and predictions were found to be possible of approaching mental upsets in hospital patients by spotting the warning signs in the field patterns. Not only humans have this electrostatic field; simpler organisms such as slime moulds and obelia, plants and trees, mice and monkeys all have their own and show cyclic changes with various environmental conditions which affect them.

Although the general features of this field seem to fit in with the response and subtlety requirements of the more dynamic and informative auras seen by some clairvoyants, it is difficult to visualise how the minimal field strengths involved could be directly responsible for modifying any radiation of electro-magnetic energy, so that an observing eye could discriminate. However, if it could be confirmed, Dr. Kilner's observation that the aura he saw was influenced by static electricity charges might be taken as a favourable indication that the electrostatic field was involved some-how.

Enough has been said to show that a wide variety of pos-sibilities can be examined in the search for evidence that there is an aura caused by some form of radiant energy. Technical means exist, or could be designed, to detect the minutest amount of radiation of any wavelength if the test-ing of some likely theory required it; but if no coherent hypothesis can be constructed to explain all the aura data or if a nul result should appear after all the tests had been completed, the answer from the physical sciences would tend to be that the aura is not of this form and must be sought elsewhere.

Hypothesis—physical phenomenon perceived psychically

It is quite possible that none of the five sense channels used by the physical body is employed at all in perceiving any of the traditional auras. Studies of extra-sensory perception (E.S.P.) in parapsychology have established that there is at least one further communication channel either used or lying latent in all human beings; this is also referred to generally by the term 'psychic faculty' which covers the whole range of processes, from perceiving something physical or non-physical by a sense which is not part of the physical body's equipment, to the final presentation of the information to the individual's conscious awareness.

Accepting the existence of an E.S.P. or psychic ability, the second hypothesis puts the idea that some physical phenomenon or state of the organism is being observed in this way although it would not be perceived by any bodily sense. The information obtained is then given in some representative form to the waking consciousness just as the electrical activities of the optic nerve are finally reconstituted into a 'visible' picture.

Suppose, for example, that the electrostatic field is one of the real aura phenomena observed as some experimenters have already suggested. The psychic sense would perceive this field as a three-dimensional object differentiated by its minute electrical potential differences; but this would be meaningless to the conscious mind unless it was presented in some way to which the individual's consciousness was already accustomed. What better method would there be of showing how a variable quantity alters its magnitude in space than to use the format of normal eyesight, namely, a picture of the space under observation with the field outlined as contours? This could presumably be in black and white with the potential differences indicated by the shades or intensities of black. Still better, would be to use the colour code already established from illumination phenomena in the physical world and present the directly observed potential differences as colour differences and intensity variations. This end result might be akin to a traditional aura and if this assumed manner of working were actually the case, verbal descriptions could then be understood in terms of their electric field origin.

The assumptions just outlined as to a natural cause of one form of aura may or may not be far from the truth but, nevertheless, the method of working described is known to be typical of the psychic and unconscious mind which is obliged to employ symbolism and pictorial imagery when there is no other way of conveying the information.

When the waking consciousness is made aware of the external world through the eyes, the same image-creating process is involved there too, only the imagery does not need to be symbolic, but instead has to bear a direct correspondence with experience. Even so, countless everyday examples occur with ordinary eyesight whereby optical illusions and mistaken appearances betray the non-factual component of vision. The psychic faculty probably uses the identical image-forming mechanism for conveying its own special kind of information and a person psychically endowed in this way may differ from one not so endowed merely in the sensitivity of perception and the degree to which normal waking consciousness can be held in abeyance during the function of the subtler process.

Hypothesis—psychological states or psychic phenomena perceived psychically

The third possible method by which an aura may be 'perceived' is logically an extension of the second, in that instead of the observer's psychic faculty perceiving a physical phenomenon, it acquaints itself with emotional, mental or psychic data by direct psychic communication with the observed.

If humans have a psychic ability, and therefore a psychic entity which exercises it, so do other forms of life albeit to a much smaller degree. In this case, like can communicate with like and whatever is known to the observed psyche is capable of being transferred to the psyche of the percipient. The information thus passed can obviously be processed and displayed pictorially to the waking consciousness as outlined before. Under this hypothesis, the real explanation for the aura will be purely in psychological or psychical terms pictorially displayed, in which case the problem has to be examined by psychological or parapsychological techniques.

Summary

If forms of aura are perceived around humans and all living things, the implications may be important within the context of theories about Man. The fact that auras have been mentioned and depicted for centuries is no proof that they exist objectively. Several sources of optical and psychological delusion are now recognised but sufficient techniques and knowledge have been gathered for these to be detected or avoided at source and for a clear decision to be made as to whether the enquiry has substance or not.

In the absence of such a firm ruling, forms of aura are assumed to exist, but of the three main possible explanations only the purely physical hypothesis of electro-magnetic radiation has received any attention and that is simply because a general understanding already exists of how to approach the problem. In addition, recording natural radiations from the body requires nothing more than the presence of the observed; but, both hypotheses involving psychic ability demand at the outset a psychic who can sustain a significant ability through many experiments. Such people are hard to find and this one difficulty is often sufficient to thwart the necessary work.

For the present, the situation is fairly wide open. Reports and stories abound, but, scientifically speaking, it is not established that auras really exist which fit the time-honoured descriptions, nor is it known whether the phenomena should be sought in domains of the physical, the psychological or the psychic. It is suspected that too much attention has been given in this account to the radiation hypothesis; except perhaps for Dr. Kilner's type of slow-moving bodily fringe aura the tendency of thought is now towards the other two theories mentioned, particularly the third, due to the difficulties of explaining the facts in terms of any electro-magnetic wavelength at all. However, it is only by working at it and uncovering the shortcomings of one idea that the urge is felt towards another and better solution.

Further reading

The Human Atmosphere (*The Aura*), by W. J. Kilner (Kegan Paul, London, 1920).

The Origin and Properties of the Human Aura, by O. Bagnall (Kegan Paul, London, 1937).

'A Review of Kilner's Work', by A. J. Ellison (*Journal of the Society for Psychical Research*, Vol. 44, March 1967).

The Next World—and the Next, by R. Crookall (Theosophical Publishing House, 1966).

The Mystery of the Human Aura, by Ursula Roberts (Marylebone Spiritualist Association, 1950).

Is etheric radiation electro-magnetic?

It has been said that, 'since most people cannot use etheric sight, the obvious assumption is that what is visible by such sight is not seen by means of what are called the visual rays but by means of ultra-violet or infra-red rays'.

It is by no means obvious, though it could be right. Why should it be assumed that etheric sight uses electro-magnetic radiation at all? There is a danger here of falling into the same trap as the scientists who assume that everything in our experience must be explicable in terms of physical phenomena. It is customary to regard the etheric as part of the physical plane and not radically different from the dense physical. It seems, however, there is a considerable line of demarcation between the etheric and dense physical levels.

We should not assume that etheric radiation can be detected by physical means. It is possible that some *correlation* exists between the ability of certain filters to transmit infra-red and etheric radiations without these two forms of radiation being *identical*. If the correlation is not complete this could explain some of the exceptions that have been noted.

Mr. Geoffrey Hodson's clairvoyant investigations into the structure of the atom have been used as a basis for discussion, but if we accept the objectivity of his clairvoyance, then it seems that his work on occult chemistry can only be interpreted as indicating that the distinction between etheric and dense physical matter is greater than has often been assumed. If the atomic structure is different then the radiation is probably different also because electro-magnetic radiation arises from the atomic structure of matter at the physical level.

It is often risky to assume that concepts which work well in one field of endeavour can *necessarily* be transferred to another or even that they apply without drastic modifications to a different range of conditions in the same field of endeavour. In the latter category we can cite the inadequacy of classical mechanics to deal with the realms of atomic physics. It is not that the more general laws of relativistic mechanics and quantum mechanics do not apply in the everyday world. The same laws hold everywhere, but different aspects of them become important under different conditions.

Biologists and psychologists like to take over the concepts and methods of physics and chemistry and believe they can explain life and mind in terms of physics and chemistry without introducing any radically new concepts such as life manifesting in, or mind functioning through, a physical body. They should, however, be able to profit from the experience of the physicists when they attempted to extrapolate accepted concepts and laws beyond their range of validity. Many people tried to interpret the unexpected result of the Michelson–Morley experiment, but it took the genius of Einstein to see that a fundamentally new approach was required.

Discussing the rapid advances being made in biochemistry at the John Curtin School of Medical Research at Canberra research workers have suggested that all bodily functions and ailments will be eventually explained in terms of chemistry. One of them could 'see the day when drugs would be made to order for every condition for every patient'.

The noted neurophysiologist, Sir John Eccles, was not so sure. He says:

> 'I should think we are about a thousand years off our goal. Man will be the last thing that man will learn. He is in the interesting philosophical position of having to use his own brain to find out how it works. It may well be impossible.
>
> 'Scientists, I think, have rendered a grave disservice to humanity by their too ready dogmatism on what man is. With no real knowledge they just brand everything they believe as knowledge, and there have been more superstitions put up by scientists about man than I would like to think. We are concerned, to my mind, with an unfathomable mystery, and it is just as well to know that in advance. Many people think the explanation of man as a clever animal or robot is just around the corner. But that doesn't go for me!'

Bergson in his book, *The Creative Mind*, speaking of science, says:

> 'Its original domain which has continued to be its preferred domain, is that of inert matter. It is less at its ease in the organised world, where it threads its way with an assured step only when it relies on physics and chemistry; it clings to the physico-chemical in vital phenomena rather than what is really vital in the living. But great is its embarrassment when it reaches the mind.'

Here are a scientist and a philosopher who do not believe that all manifestation can be explained along the lines of physics and chemistry and of course there are many others. Theosophists have a great opportunity to develop this theme, but we should be the last to assume that physical laws can *necessarily* be applied to the superphysical, and the writer regards the etheric as superphysical. The transition from dense physical to etheric seems to be of a different order altogether from transition between say solid, liquid and gas. Were it not so the existence of the etheric would probably be common scientific knowledge.

Levels of consciousness

Early theosophical textbooks describe six planes besides the physical, each composed of superphysical matter increasing in tenuity to the highest levels. The planes are supposed to interpenetrate one another in the same space, except that the higher ones extend out beyond the earth's atmosphere. Nevertheless, in lists and diagrams the planes were always represented one above the other and it was customary to speak of upper or higher planes in contrast to the lower.

These somewhat materialistic ideas have undergone evolution, and modern theosophists more often speak of the corresponding levels of consciousness, each with its own characteristic quality. Moreover, the terms higher and lower tend to be replaced by inner and outer. More important, the old diagram has given way to the more evocative one shown below, in which the levels are interleaved, with the old 'form planes' on the left and the 'life planes' on the right, to illustrate their intimate interrelationship. This permits logical division into the broader segments one can appreciate in experience, corresponding roughly with the Christian body, soul and spirit. This version of the diagram does not conflict seriously with the ideas of modern psychology, but its more detailed analytical subdivision, within a coherent whole, may contribute to better understanding of human nature.

It is not really possible to describe and classify affairs of the spirit accurately in words, but what better way is there? The English equivalents used in place of the original Sanskrit terms to name the various levels of consciousness must not be taken too literally; still less the words used to suggest the qualities of all the levels placed on the left of the diagram compared with those on the right. Such terms are used evocatively rather than descriptively; they can be understood not so much directly and separately by the mind, as by brooding over the picture as a whole until one 'gets the feel of it'.

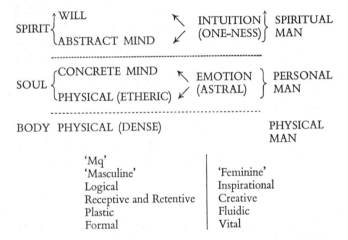

If this is done, the relevance of the diagram will appear at many points in the course of this book. At this stage, it will be used only to illustrate the relationships between the etheric and dense physical levels. Formerly, the solid, liquid and gaseous sub-levels of the physical were supposed to continue smoothly into the supergaseous etheric, which is said to be concerned among other things with the health and vitality aspects of the body. On this basis it seemed likely that etheric matter should be detectable sooner or later by scientific instruments. The new diagram suggests a different situation. It will be noticed that both the mental and physical levels are subdivided into sub-levels with distinctly different qualities, and that the lines separating body, soul and spirit occur just at these points of subdivision. From the human point of view the distinction between etheric and physical is particularly sharp, for the former is a level to which consciousness extends, whereas it is held that human consciousness has no direct contact at all with the dense physical, the body being merely a vehicle which it uses as a tool. On this basis it is understandable why the writer of the previous paper doubts if the etheric and its radiations will affect physical scientific instruments however sensitive.

Photography and etheric radiation

One cannot help feeling that a certain ampunt of confusion may be creeping into the minds of some people over the matter of etheric photographs and similar matters. We should make some clear distinctions.

1. The de la Warr–Corte photographs taken on un-exposed, fully wrapped plates, should be seen, *not* as photographs of any etheric structure or field, but as projections of thought-forms in the operator's mind.[1] These thoughts come from three sources; one of these is the result of psychometry of blood or other specimens; another, the operator's own self-produced thoughts; and thirdly, the suggestions put to him by others—sometimes, for experimental purposes, deliberately to mislead.

2. The findings of Brigadier Firebrace and his group, that the Corte camera is superfluous should be borne in mind. It seems that the actual 'camera'—i.e. the photographic apparatus which focuses images on the film, is simply the etheric of the operator, which has special qualities. In view of the Firebrace work, it would be worth studying his findings very thoroughly, before embarking on the task of making apparatus which may be quite futile and intrinsically useless for the purpose.

During the period 1935–1937 several members of the Science Group of the Theosophical Research Centre met regularly for photographic experiments aimed at photo-graphing the aura around the human hand. Long-exposure infra-red photographs of a hand held some distance in front of a dull black background showed signs of a mist surrounding the hand. However, this effect appeared to be due to halation (fogging by light reflected from the rear surface of the plate). This was confirmed by including a white cardboard hand in the field, and this also showed a strong 'aura'; also by covering the human hand with a black cardboard mask, when no sign of aura appeared.

In later experiments ultra-violet light was used, either from a quartz mercury vapour lamp with a filter to exclude visible light, or from a high-voltage quartz mercury–neon lamp emitting almost exclusively monochromatic ultra-violet at 254 mμ. A camera with a quartz lens was used, and also a reflecting camera with surface-silvered mirrors. None of these photographs revealed any trace of aura round the hand. Similar negative results were obtained when the short-wave ultra-violet light was used to make shadow-graphs of the hand. Evidently the photographic emulsion is still too insensitive an instrument to record the etheric directly, unless it is densified by a medium into ectoplasm.

[1]*Light*, March 1957.

SECTION IV

Psychometry

Fossils come to life

A psychometrive investigation into a chapter in primate evolution

Introduction

A considerable volume of experimental work by para-psychologists has established a strong case for the validity of clairvoyance as a human faculty. This does not imply that any statement supposedly obtained by clairvoyance must be accepted; what has been established with a considerable level of certainty is merely that clairvoyance can provide accurate information. Indeed, much of the information of a scientific nature which was provided by the very highly regarded Theosophical clairvoyants A. Besant and C. Leadbeater has been seriously questioned. Their work on occult chemistry has been closely examined in recent years by scientists competent in the field concerned. The conclusion appears to be that very slight correspondence exists between the clair-voyant results and those of modern scientific studies on the nature and properties of matter. Their studies on human evolution and history appear to have been far less closely examined. The information provided by the Secret Doctrine and the Besant–Leadbeater investigations appears to be highly incompatible with the views of modern scientific students of mammalian and human evolution.

The studies of parapsychologists have suggested that the clairvoyant faculty as they have met it is somewhat fugitive and erratic. In this paper we are not concerned with the acceptability or otherwise of the general body of occult information, but rather with the reliability of the developed clairvoyant faculty as a research tool. Independent investigations of the latter are particularly desirable. It is unfortunate, however, that some serious—and subtle—difficulties exist in such investigations which make it very difficult, if not impossible, to obtain conclusive results.

Material and method

We were most fortunate in having for this investigation the co-operation of the well known clairvoyant Mr. Geoffrey Hodson, of New Zealand. The material chosen for investigation was fossil remains of australopithecines, or 'ape-men' from South Africa. These interesting creatures lived about half a million years ago. They were man-like in being entirely erect-walking, with an anatomical structure closely resembling that of man; but were ape-like chiefly in possessing a brain of ape size.

An initial 'pilot' investigation was carried out by sending two isolated teeth to Mr. Hodson in New Zealand. These had the catalogue numbers and any other means of identification removed, and were simply labelled A and B. A short series of noncommital questions accompanied the specimens to indicate the type of information required. The actual investigations were carried out, and fully recorded on tape, in the home of Dr. D. Lyness of Whangarei, New Zealand. Copies of the tapes were sent to us in South Africa and transcribed. The records thus consist of the full tape record and a typed transcript thereof.

A second series of specimens was then sent, consisting of four teeth of four different individuals and a quartz flake. These were dealt with in the same fashion. The results were

sufficiently interesting for an opportunity to be made for
Mr. Hodson to visit South Africa to allow for a fuller series
of investigations to be carried out.

The procedure in the South African series of investigations was essentially the same: teeth or other specimens
labelled with a noncommittal symbol were handed to Mr.
Hodson, who described his observations aloud, the entire
proceedings being recorded on tape. In this case, five
periods of investigation were carried out at Sterkfontein,
one of the sites from which australopithecine material was
excavated. Two were carried out in a private home in
Johannesburg, some twenty-five miles from Sterkfontein.

The procedure was as follows: the clairvoyant lay full
length on his back and closed his eyes. The microphone of
the tape recorder was placed on his chest or suspended at a
convenient distance. The recording operator sat as far away
as the cord permitted (roughly 5 feet), while the senior
author sat further away with the specimens to hand, and
made notes of any points of interest. After an interval of
approximately 3 to 10 minutes, small involuntary muscular
movements became apparent in the clairvoyant. Usually at
this stage he asked for the specimen, which he then placed on
his forehead a little above the root of the nose. After a
further period of time he would indicate that he was ready,
the recorder was started and the observations, spoken aloud,
recorded. The interval between lying down and the start of
recording ranged from 5 to 15 minutes. In the normal
course of events the clairvoyant did not see the specimen
with physical vision before or during the investigation. It
was noted that before the start of an investigation the clairvoyant seemed a little restless and at the close, quiet and
sometimes tired. It was possible at all stages of an investiga-

tion to converse normally with the clairvoyant, and many questions were put to him in such a way as to elicit specific information without at the same time giving away facts which seem subsequently to have emerged from the investigation. In the normal course of an investigation no information was volunteered about a specimen, nor about the australopithecines in general; and the two investigators— in one case, one only—present with the clairvoyant adopted a passive and neutral mental attitude as far as was feasible. At no time during the entire series of investigations was there discussion about australopithecines with the clairvoyant: an outline of the scientific information available about them was given after the series had been completed. In only two instances was this routine departed from and these will be discussed later.

The considerable footage of taped record was transcribed verbatim, and from the typed record thus obtained all definite statements were extracted and arranged under four headings:

1. Statements which could be checked against existing scientific evidence, and which are correct.
2. Statements which are probably correct according to indirect scientific evidence.
3. Statements which can be checked against existing scientific evidence, and which are wrong.
4. Statements which cannot at present be checked scientifically, and the accuracy of which is therefore unknown.

A second analysis was done—according to which only those statements were extracted, for each particular specimen investigated, which indicated clearly whether the specimen had been correctly identified. Furthermore, as in some instances the same specimen was given for investigation on more than one occasion, comparisons were made between the separate sets of results obtained from the same investigation after it had been completed, the clairvoyant often seemed unclear about the details of his observation—that is, he did not seem to remember very well what he had said.

Results

During the investigations the clairvoyant gave an impression —which can readily be checked on the original tapes—of great objectivity and care in observation. From his manner, a clear impression was also given of actually observing a scene and reporting on it. He spoke confidently—not that this implies that a ready answer was available for every question, or that an attitude of knowing all about the matter was apparent; but that there was no evidence of confusion or impreciseness. When a question was asked, the clairvoyant would usually say that he must first look again to see what the answer was, and then described the detail asked for; or say that the creature being observed was standing in such a way that the observation could not be made for the moment —and then later, perhaps after going on to something else, say that the creature had turned so that the feature was now observable and then proceed to describe it.

On being questioned closely while not actually investigating some detail, the clairvoyant explained that, having achieved the correct state for making the observations, it was as though he was looking through a tube in his head and observing an animated scene in full colour at the end of the tube. If observing conditions reached the optimum, then the effect was that of passing down the tube so that the field of observation expanded and became unrestricted.

To illustrate the vividly realistic character of the clair-voyant's experience, there follows a brief excerpt from one of the sessions, faithfully transcribed from the tape recording. He was handed a fossil tooth from one of the prehistoric creatures, which served to transport him back in time, so that he seemed to be actually present at episodes in the creature's life.

First impressions . . . of the psychology of the apparent owner of this tooth. He is—it is crude, capable of a snarling ferocity, and excited anger. It is not eating this time; I am looking at it in profile. It's definitely man-like, however primitively so—it's . . . there it is. . . . Got a profile which shows a raised nose. It—it is—it's got a skull which is man-like, rounded, very low on the forehead. It's not far from the ape; there are some very ape-like attributes, I think, but it's got a man's 'soul' or psychology, predominant over pure sub-human animality. Its nose isn't very much raised, but it is raised—not flat. Its eyes are round; I see them rather well. Small, but good eyes— good-looking eyes; they're deep-set as I said, same thing I think, same creature; hairy—lot of hair—forehead—very hairy eyebrows; that ridge that I've spoken of before. The eyebrow hair is rough and long.

The transcripts and even the tabulated analyses are too long to reproduce in an article such as this. It is therefore possible to give only the main conclusions emerging from the analyses. The scientific problem which was investi-gated is distinctly complex: no less than three closely related man-like creatures occupied a small portion of a small valley near Sterkfontein over a geologically brief period of time, approximately half a million years ago. Two of these creatures were fairly similar, while the other was much less man-like and more ape-like. The evidence indicates that one of the more man-like alone occupied the valley at the beginning of the period represented by the known material. Later, the most man-like one (in fact an early true man) moved into the area and displaced the other. A little later, consistent with increasingly moist climatic conditions, the most ape-like form moved into the valley and occupied it jointly with the most man-like form. The very ape-like form was a vegetarian; its companion an omivore; and the third form apparently mainly carnivorous.

With one exception all identifications in the series were quite accurate, each of the three forms being correctly identified, whether they were the primary objects of investigation at the time, or were merely a creature observed in the environment of one under investigation. The exception referred to occurred in the very first 'pilot' investigation in New Zealand on two teeth. The two forms represented by the teeth were described at length, and quite accurately as far as verifying evidence exists, but each was described from the tooth representing the other type.

The detailed descriptions were accurate as far as evidence exists which allowed checking. This applied not only to anatomical detail, such as whether canine teeth protruded beyond the other teeth, the presence or not of skull crests, presence or not of a definite forehead or chin, whether the bridge of the nose was raised or not, posture, nature of the hands and feet etc., but also to behaviour, diet, etc, in no instance was a demonstrably incorrect statement made. Whether the statements which could not be checked against scientific evidence are correct cannot, of course, be determined. In one instance a specimen was given with the simple request for identification and manner in which the individual met his death—a usual request. The clairvoyant immediately on speaking indicated that the individual had died a violent death as an adolescent, after being attacked in a manner which included severe head injury. Both the immature age and the head injury were facts known from scientific evidence, since open skull sutures proved the first; and two peculiar depressed fractures in the parietal region, which from their nature must have been inflicted about the time of death, proved the second. But these were not seen by the clairvoyant, since the specimen was brought out and handed to him while he had his eyes closed. The description of the two types of creatures involved in the fracas which caused the death of the individual concerned was accurate for the two forms known to occur at the site which yielded the specimen.

Many similar instances could be quoted if space permitted. We must content ourselves with stating that the degree of detailed observation regarding the animals, their behaviour and the environment in which they lived was very considerable and very accurate where checking was possible— which was the case for roughly half of the statements made. Where the same specimen was investigated more than once, among a different constellation of specimens on each occasion, there were no discrepancies between different sets of observations made on the same specimen on different days.

Discussion

On the face of it the results obtained indicate a high degree of reliability of the clairvoyant powers of the subject in this series of investigations. A large amount of information was provided about creatures which have long been extinct, and

with which the subject was not familiar. The amount of
scientific information on this topic now available is very
considerable, and serves to show that all statements made by
the clairvoyant which could be checked are correct, whether
referring to broad outlines or anatomical minutiae.

However, this type of investigation is notoriously difficult,
as the parapsychologists have discovered, because of the
difficulty of demonstrating that the information was
obtained by clairvoyance alone. Closer scrutiny of the
results is consequently necessary.

In the first place there is the one apparent error: the trans-
posed descriptions in the case of the initial trial on two
specimens in New Zealand. This is puzzling. In view of the
many other instances where no error was made, it is tempting to think that unwittingly an error was made somewhere
along the line in the records. At this stage this can be neither
proved nor disproved—as the records stand the descriptions
of the creatures concerned are correct, but the actual identifications are wrong.

The main problem is to eliminate the possibility that the
accuracy of the results obtained is due, not to clairvoyance,
but to telepathy. That is to say that the results were not
derived from the specimen by clairvoyance but from the
brain or mind of someone who had accurate information
about the known scientific evidence. It may be said at once
that much of the information produced by the clairvoyant
during the investigations had never been in the mind of the
author until mentioned by the clairvoyant. However, this
in most cases means nothing since at this stage we do not
know whether that information is correct. If incorrect, this
fact would tend to support a telepathic explanation; if
correct, it would discount such an explanation and be good

presumptive evidence of pure clairvoyance. Several statements made by the clairvoyant are of interest from this point of view.

The first involves a stone implement which was stated to have been involved in earth movement and to have had water running over it. Although in the course of excavation evidence was found which showed that two major collapses had occurred at this site, there had been no conscious thought at any stage that the specimen here involved was now lying in a different position after such a collapse. More significantly, it was not known at the time of this investigation that this particular stone implement was one that had come from a zone of decomposed rock. The decomposition is due to the leaching action of water. The excavation records were consulted after the investigation, and only then was it consciously thought that indeed it must have had water moving over it at some stage over quite a long period.

Two further cases are of a different character. In one, a specimen was given to the clairvoyant without any information about it being volunteered. But during the investigation of it, a deliberate attempt to confuse the issue was made by the senior author who spent the time creating as vivid thought images as possible of one of the three creatures *not* represented by the specimen being investigated. This had no effect upon the results; and on subsequent questioning the clairvoyant said that the images he had got from the specimen—which were correct as far as available evidence goes—were quite clear and not confused by other images. In another investigation, towards the end of the series, this attempt to put the clairvoyant on to the wrong track was taken even further by deliberately giving erroneous information about the identity of the specimen when it was

handed over for investigation, and then also attempting to
hold an unbroken mental image, consistent with the wrong
information given, during the whole course of the investigation. The first image obtained was the correct one, but was
rejected as wrong by the clairvoyant because it did not agree
with what he had been led to expect. He then got another
image—of a form occurring at the same site—but the first,
and correct, image kept recurring until the clairvoyant said
that he had no option but to study it. When asked if the
confusion could not be cleared up, he tried again and then
said that he had to conclude that it was not the form which
he had been told it should be, but the other one. Hence, in
spite of material efforts to mislead the clairvoyant, he still
arrived at the correct conclusion.

In the case of the latter two specimens, it may be argued
that even though wrong mental images were strongly held
in order to attempt to mislead the clairvoyant, the right
information was also present in the mind of a person present
at the time. This is true, and since the whole process of
telepathy is obscure and it is not known from what level of
the mind it works, one cannot be sure whether the one
mental image would have been more potent than the other.
But it is difficult to see, since the original information and
the spurious image both originate as definite thoughts in the
mind, why the clairvoyant should accept one and not the
other if he has no external standard against which to judge
them. Almost half of the information given by the clairvoyant also could not have been derived from the mind
of anyone other than the clairvoyant himself. Finally, the
cautious and apparently highly objective nature of the
observations and their great internal consistency seem to us
to argue in favour of the conclusion that none of the

information was telepathically obtained. The records are very extensive and the investigations shuttled backwards and forwards without pattern from one sort of creature to another. If this information was not coming from some definite and accurate source, it is hardly conceivable that someone quite unfamiliar with the scientific field concerned could have produced such a mass of information which is internally perfectly consistent for the anatomy, behaviour and environment of three different creatures. It would appear that the clairvoyant was tapping some sound source of knowledge, which created the appearance to him of actually being present witnessing the lives of the creatures concerned, and which had no relation to the minds of any other persons. What this source of information was is not scientifically determinable at the present time.

Commentary on Fossils come to life

One's first response to these investigations must be to marvel at their accuracy, and to compliment Mr. Hodson upon his remarkable psychic abilities. It can be argued that the technique actually employed was telepathy, rather than psychometry or clairvoyance through time, as the observer believed: but the fact remains that *irrespective* of the source of the visions they could only have been obtained by some psychic means stimulated by the objects presented, and almost all of those that could be checked were correct. This work is therefore in another class altogether from the familiar experiments in telepathy and card-guessing, in which the observer is *usually wrong*, and scores are only slightly above chance, e.g. anything over 20% of answers correct, with the usual five cards. Such experiments, repeated on innumerable occasions, have sufficed to establish the reality of E.S.P. to the satisfaction of most people who have studied the facts. How much more convincing, however, is the present work, which does not depend in any degree upon statistical analysis. Mr. Hodson leaves us in no doubt about his psychic powers. It is against this background that their precise nature may be discussed.

Many among the older generation of readers familiar with Leadbeater's books, will have no hesitation in accepting Hodson's work as an example of genuine clairvoyance. It should be mentioned, therefore, that some members of the Science Group are disposed to give more credence to the highly critical work of the Society for Psychical Research, and to investigations of E.S.P. by university groups, notably at Duke University. Most of these people regard telepathy as the *only* psychic faculty that is scientifically established and respectable. One might think that acceptance of one psychic faculty would make it easier for them to accept others, but the reverse is true. They find no indisputable evidence for them that cannot be explained away by some form of telepathy, even though they sometimes seem to be straining at the gnat of clairvoyance while swallowing the camel of precognitive telepathy, i.e. receiving in advance a thought that is not yet in anyone's mind. One member suggests that if this is acceptable, then why not postcognitive telepathy also, i.e. the idea that the seer tuned in to the thoughts of the long-dead ape-men themselves. If their thoughts assumed pictorial forms, this would not be very different from what the seer supposed he was doing. Other members were convinced that the seer was merely reading the mind of the author, while others again, though inclined to this view, wisely reserved a final judgement. Experiments were suggested that might establish the reality of clairvoyance objectively; these will be discussed in later sections of this book.

Clearly if the seer obtained his facts from the investigator's mind, then the work would still be of great interest as a good example of telepathy, but it would have contributed nothing new to archeology. It is necessary here to comment on the details of the scenes 'seen' by Mr. Hodson, which were certainly not in the conscious mind of the author. There is a naïve tendency to suppose that since the checkable facts proved correct, then very likely the others were also; unfortunately this has to be questioned. Work with mediums and psychics of the more usual negative type has shown that the unconscious mind has an astonishing propensity for dramatisation. As in dreaming, it can devise purely imaginary scenes at great speed and in convincing detail. It seems fairly certain that most of the material produced by mediums arises in this way, even though they may be convinced of its external origin. Whether a positive psychic can avoid being tricked by this unconscious dramatisation is simply not known at present, and unfortunately one cannot necessarily accept the seer's belief that he understands the workings of his subconscious mind, any more than the rest of us do.

With this explanation, parts of the long discussion provoked in the Science Group *Journal* by this work can be presented. The material is rearranged to bring together all the arguments and counter-arguments on a particular point. Besides general comments, all the discussion ranged over just two aspects of the investigation, namely the 'discovery' of previously unconsidered facts about the South African prehistoric creatures, and the attempts deliberately to mislead the psychic. To avoid confusion it is necessary to distinguish the authors of the separate comments, and this will be done by the letters A, B and C.

(A) It is very important in connection with experiments such as those described by the authors to realise (as they are well aware) that the explanation of the results is as yet unknown. The work is at the fact-finding stage. It is very tempting for the theosophical reader to speak of 'akashic records', 'ajna chakras' and 'higher levels', etc., but this is not very helpful because the words have no precise and generally accepted meaning and may lead one astray. Spiritualists who sometimes use psychometry as 'proof of survival' interpret the results in terms of communication of facts about the object from a discarnate entity to the psychic. The old-style theosophist tends to speak of akashic records, etc. The psychic's own explanation of the faculty is also a function of the way he was 'trained', i.e. of what he was told about his experiences by others. It is clear, therefore, that scientific workers must, at this stage, record facts, and make them as clear and unambiguous as possible. The formulation of theories will come later.

Certain facts regarding psychic perception have already been established beyond reasonable doubt. Coincident, retrocognitive and precognitive telepathy have been established as facts in nature, i.e. one mind can sometimes know something which is, has been, or will be, in another mind, without the intervention of any of the five senses. And the relationship between the minds involved is at the *unconscious* level. Information acquired by the unconscious mind of one person from that of another (if there is, in fact, separation at that level) may be presented to the conscious mind in one or more of several ways. A voice may be heard subjectively (termed 'clairaudience'), a picture (sometimes symbolic) may be seen (termed 'clairvoyance') or a feeling or 'hunch' may be felt (termed 'clairsentience').

The author mentioned a description by the psychic of water running at one time over the stone implement under examination. This possibility had not occurred to the author who was, however, later able to deduce it as probably true by means of other data acquired at the site where the implement was found. In this case it may be suggested that the author's unconscious mind (vastly greater than the conscious) had already noted the facts not consciously observed and had drawn the appropriate conclusions—to be picked up by the psychic and dramatised accordingly. The unconscious is very clever at sorting out facts and drawing conclusions, as most people discover when they 'sleep on' a problem and are presented with the solution in the morning.

(B) The author seems to have overlooked a factor which, from a scientific viewpoint, vitiates all the work done on archaeological material: if *anybody* has examined this material and has formed even a tentative idea of its origin, etc., why should Mr. Hodson not have been psychometrising these ideas rather than the actual history of the object, and embroidering on the theme of the ideas impressed on it in its more *recent* history?

(C) Quite obviously, the high score of successes cannot be accounted for by chance, and some extra-sensory faculty is in evidence. In view of the presence of the investigator, the first thought that comes to mind is that we are seeing a first-rate example of telepathy. Even if this was a complete answer, it would still have been a worth-while investigation. But there were many instances where 'new' information was given by the clairvoyant. It might be argued that out of the many people who must have examined the specimens, at least one of them gave a passing thought to the idea Mr. Hodson presented, and therefore it could still have been telepathy.

But what about the many instances in which the scientifically correct answer was known? In these cases too, there must have been many other possibilities held in the consciousness of some individuals; so how was it that Mr. Hodson picked out the correct 'authoritative' answers from the welter of ideas? An explanation which maintains that Mr. Hodson telepathically contacted the authoritative answers in those cases where this answer was correct, but in others switched to non-authoritative passing thoughts seems singularly unconvincing. It seems that psychometry may well be inherently more reliable than 'straight' clairvoyance. It may indeed be regarded as a form of telepathy, but post-telepathy, not current or precognitive telepathy. One wonders if the passing thoughts of the ape-men themselves can properly be excluded entirely in this connection.

The author replied as follows to these three comments:

'There is a strong tendency among these critics to explain all observations in terms of telepathy—which explanations sometimes have to be somewhat far-fetched. This is the case with the australopithecine specimens where hundreds of people have thought about and handled the specimens, with the thoughts concerned ranging from the ridiculous to the factually correct. Why should telepathy just happen to provide the correct selection of information from the available large and very mixed bag? In some cases all the information could not have been got from one mind, thus implying that when operating in this manner the psychic's faculty is ranging about among a number of minds. Finally, precognition has to be brought in to explain the cases where the first mention of an item of information comes from the psychic. One may then argue that, having been mentioned by the psychic, it is in the minds of other persons, from whom the psychic can then be held to have got it by precognition to explain his having mentioned it in the first place! In the light of the evidence from parapsychology it is much more reasonable to think in terms of clairvoyance being the faculty involved rather than telepathy.'

(B) I am afraid I cannot take very seriously the investigator's attempts to blot out his own thoughts: it is rather naïve to say to the psychometrist, 'I'm going to try and mislead you by telling you that this object is X, while I really believe it to by Y': yet that is precisely what it amounts to. Any knowledge of the human mind would have shown the futility of such an attempt to deceive.

(A) It may be suggested that there was little point in creating strong images in the conscious mind of one of the experimenters of a kind designed to mislead the psychic. It is in the *un*conscious that any telepathy which may be occurring takes place, and there we do not know how to control it. It *may* have been the case that the psychic acquired from the experimenter at the unconscious mind level the information about the specimens presented, and the psychic's unconscious mind 'dramatised' it in the well-known way, and produced the pictures seen and described.

The author replied as follows:

'These critics take too simple a view of the matter. First, it would appear that the thoughts of the conscious mind are not to be discounted entirely in respect of telepathy. This is shown by the fact that the most successful and stringent experiments on telepathy have used as a target a subject holding successively a series of mental images in his conscious mind. However telepathy functions, the thoughts of the conscious mind somehow or another have some bearing on it. Secondly, since it is axiomatic in experimental work that all avenues must be explored and that ones which appear to conflict with preconceived notions should not be ignored, the attempted deception was undertaken simply to see what, if any, information would result. However, it should be realised that the situation was not quite as simple as might appear. The deception was attempted towards the end of the series of investigations at a stage when the psychic had come to trust the experimenters not to try any tricks on him. At this point the false information was *verbally* given to him quite casually when a new specimen was handed to him partway through a session. An attempt was made to support the wrong impression given verbally by thinking strongly about the creature which the author had said the specimen belonged to and which is one that had actually lived in that area and had been investigated by the psychic on previous occasions. In other words the mind (conscious and unconscious) of the author had any amount of genuine information in it about the creature which the psychic had been led to understand he was dealing with. Furthermore, the deception *did* have an effect since the correct information came at once to the mind of the psychic, but he rejected it because of what he had been told. It was only because the actually correct but apparently wrong image kept obtruding and after an explanation was asked for of why it kept presenting itself, that the psychic re-examined his identification and decided on the correct image. Finally, the psychic was unaware of the deception until he was informed of it after the investigation. It seems to us that if the psychic was in fact simply getting the information from the mind of the author, then the deception could very easily have succeeded because the psychic had thus far experienced no deceptive tactics and was therefore not expecting any and the incorrect information was not artificial but had an extensive genuine background in the mind of a person present and had direct relevance to the situation being investigated.'

The last word goes to one of the commentators, then each reader must form his own personal conclusions from the conflicting opinions.

(A) Concerning the experiment in which incorrect information was given to the psychic, it is difficult to understand the author's reasoning that 'the deception *did* have an effect since the correct information came at once to the mind of the psychic; but he rejected it because of what he had been told. This would appear to support the view that the deception had *no* effect on the *psychic* faculty, in that the correct information came at once, as usual. It was rejected by the psychic's *conscious* mind as a result of the misleading information given. This supports the view that the information was being dramatised by the unconscious mind of the psychic, the unconscious mind of the author and that of the psychic both knowing very well the *true* nature of the specimen presented.

In trying to answer the question, 'Why should telepathy just happen to provide the correct selection of information from the available large and very mixed bag?', it is important to realise that the unconscious is not just a murky pool full of odd memories, it is vastly the greater part of our minds, with enormous powers (of intuition, etc.) which as yet we know little about. All the evidence of modern psychology surely indicates that our 'greater self' largely unfettered by space and time, may sometimes be reached through, or in, the 'unconscious'. Normally inaccessible to us in our conscious daily life, it still occasionally breaks through into consciousness—often during sleep, or in the mystical experience—and gives us evidence of the greatest wisdom. With this conception of the unconscious it is surely not surprising that it can choose the correct facts from someone else's memory store, and present them to the conscious mind in the form of pictures or symbols.

Telepathy

Telepathy—a symposium

I. THE TELEPATHY FACTOR IN EXTRA–SENSORY PERCEPTION

Telepathy is 'The communication of impressions of any kind from one mind to another, independently of the recognised channels of sense'. Telepathy has been proved to exist, both in the form of spontaneous examples between individuals, and in the form of completely controlled, statistically analysed laboratory experiments. There is no doubt whatever that some individuals can sometimes know what is in the mind of someone else without their getting to know in any normal way. And there is little doubt that this telepathic linkage is in the part of the mind of which we are not normally conscious. Telepathy does not occur consciously; it occurs outside the conscious levels of the mind and the result then pops up into consciousness.

Experiments on telepathy have been described by S. G. Soal and F. Bateman in *Modern Experiments in Telepathy* (Faber, 1954). In such experiments the 'percipient' tries to guess a series of cards which are being looked at in turn by the 'agent' in another room. Some mediums who have taken part in these trials have 'guides' who claim to be able to see into the physical world. Their information can come by clairaudience (the medium 'hearing' the name of the card spoken) or by clairvoyance (the medium 'seeing' the card in front of her 'inner eye'). Other mediums do not consider they have a 'guide', but they too have similar experiences.

The point to be made is this: the *'theory' the psychic has about how she gets the card bears little relevance to the truth of her guess*. The rate of scoring by psychics who 'see' the cards or are 'shown' them, or 'told' what they are, is not, in general, any higher than it is for those people who just 'guess', i.e. state their 'hunches'. The guesses in both cases are usually wrong, and a statistical evaluation has to be made of a large number of trials. The percipient does not usually know at the time whether any particular guess is right or wrong. It is, however, worth mentioning that sometimes, during a run of very high scoring, the percipient experiences an elevated feeling of infallibility.

In card-guessing experiments, the results obtained by Dr. Soal, and also by Dr. Rhine, show odds of many billions to one against pure chance being the only factor involved, this is, moreover, not due to faults in statistical theory. Dr. Burton H. Cramp, the President of the American Institute of Mathematical Statistics, states:

'Dr. Rhine's investigations have two aspects: experimental and statistical. On the experimental side mathematicians have of course nothing to say. On the statistical side, however, recent mathematical work has established the fact that, assuming that the experiments have been properly performed, the statistical analysis is essentially valid. If the Rhine investigation is to be fairly attacked it must be on grounds other than mathematical methods.'

Extra-sensory perception

Extra-sensory perception (E.S.P.) is perception without the use of any of the five senses, and includes all the psychic faculties, clairvoyance, clairaudience, clairsentience, and also accurs in the form, for example, of involuntary movement of a hazel twig to indicate the presence of water or of sticking of the finger on the radionic 'black box' indicator. All of these, as does telepathy, have their origin in the unconscious mind.

It appears that at the level of the mind of which we are not normally conscious in our physical waking life there is a section that behaves as if it were a creature living with us. Let us call him 'George'; in earlier theosophical books he was spoken of as the mental elemental. George has psychic powers. He can find out what is going on in other people's minds. He can find out whether there is water in the ground at our feet. Having obtained this information by E.S.P. he can sometimes tell us of his findings by pushing information up into the conscious part of the mind. It is he who works the muscles that move the hazel twig, by-passing the part of the brain that normally does this sort of thing consciously. The results both of information acquired from someone else —telepathically—and of information acquired by extrasensory means from the world around, can be impressed upon the conscious mind by 'George'. See p. 44, but we cannot tell where the information *originated*.

The following examples will illustrate the nature of E.S.P., first as explained in theosophical literature and secondly the *modus operandi* of 'George', and some modern alternative explanations of these cases.

Example 1. Many psychics have produced apparent evidence of survival of death through the use of clairvoyance and clairaudience—the evidence apparently coming from the people we call dead. The traditional explanation is that the dead people come in their astral bodies and the psychic sees and hears them through her own astral sense organs. This information is transmitted through the etheric bridge into the physical brain. The sitter is then informed, and recognises the information as coming from the discarnate relative.

Example 2. Some psychics can apparently see into closed boxes, or inside the bodies of patients for medical diagnosis. Often they obtain information on a patient's internal state which is verified by the doctor in charge. There are three rather mixed traditional explanations given here. The first speaks of an etheric retina situated a little behind the ordinary retina of the eye. This is said to be used for seeing the etheric double of the patient, where the disease is said to start. The second explanation from tradition speaks of the frontal chakram or 'third eye'. The third explanation says that the information is acquired at a 'higher level of consciousness' and is then brought down to the physical brain.

Example 3. Chemical atoms are examined and described. The book *Occult Chemistry* by A. Besant and C. W. Leadbeater is full of drawings of atoms. These are described as having been obtained by the use of the frontal chakram again, which is said to have a magnifying feature. The psychics who did this pioneering work—well before the days when we knew as much as we do now about these matters—said that they brought the atoms to rest by the use of will power, and then examined them by, as it were, pushing the magnifying lens of the frontal chakram in among the atoms and looking.

Suppose we suggested to a psychic exercising one or more of the powers in the examples just described that the results

L

might be explained by telepathy. Usually they would be not a little annoyed and refuse to work with us. Mediums who consider they are talking to the dead are angry if doubt is cast on their explanations. If they happen to be theosophists of the old tradition they will probably say that *they* can tell the difference between an astral entity and a thought form. Only very incompetent psychics get confused in this way.

Some features of the unconscious mind must now be explained, and that really means describing the ways in which 'George' (that obliging creature who is living with us) behaves. First, the 'dramatising faculty' of the unconscious mind must be considered.

'George' will do almost anything to oblige the experimenter if he can. 'George' is very useful indeed when well trained (after all, it is he who twists the hazel twig in water divining), but he needs very careful watching because he can be very misleading.

If you are anxious to communicate with someone in the next world and you go to see a medium, her 'George' is quite capable of discovering your wishes, acquiring the facts you want from *your* mind (the unconscious part containing the memories) and then dressing them up as if from a communicator; this deceives both the medium and you. Dr. S. G. Soal describes the character of John Ferguson, who 'communicated' with him through the medium Mrs. Blanche Cooper and confirmed one by one the unspoken conjectures made about him by Soal. Eventually it became clear that John Ferguson was no 'communicator', but a mere figment of the unconscious, and he disappeared at once. Week by week he had appeared at each sitting, strong and confident, never making statements that conflicted with his earlier ones and with a subtle answer ready for any attempt to trap him. The object of all this unconscious collaboration between medium and sitter was clearly to deceive the conscious mind of the sitter, who was anxious to obtain a genuine communication which could not be explained away as a case of telepathy from his own mind.

Mr. W. B. Yeats—the poet—had the plot of a play he was working on given to him *as factual* through Miss Geraldine Cummins, the automatic writing medium.

Telepathy, then, is the acquirement of information by the unconscious from other people, and its transfer into the psychic's conscious mind so that he becomes aware of it. It appears perhaps in the form of a hallucination or of a voice. The psychic, does not know where the information came from originally—how can he?—so he interprets what he experiences in accordance with the way he was taught. Some theosophists and others tend to talk about astral bodies, thought forms and many other things, as though they were objective realities, existing in our space and made of some fine material. So far there are only the statements of others to support these views, but it is not suggested that all traditional views are wrong. It is just that there are alternative explanations, which may be correct.

It should now be clear what the alternative explanations are for those specimens of E.S.P. described at the beginning.

Example 1. Communication with the dead by clairvoyance and clairaudience. 'George' gets the facts from the sitter's mind and dresses them up to appear as if from a communicator.

Example 2. Seeing inside patients in medical diagnosis. 'George' could easily get the state of affairs from the mind of the doctor in charge and dramatise it so that the psychic *thinks* she is looking inside the patient and getting the information that way.

Example 3. Chemical atoms are examined in detail. Dr. Besant and Mr. Leadbeater—great pioneers in this work—looked at certain chemical elements in the way I described and so verified a theory of Sir William Crookes about the periodic table. That theory has later been proved faulty. Could this not be an example of 'George'—two 'Georges' in collaboration—dramatising the desired information and making the experimenters think they were looking at the atoms? Whereas they were perhaps looking at thought images created by Sir William Crookes. Even people with advanced psychic powers need to eliminate the possibility of telepathic communication when arranging their clairvoyant researches.

Almost any of the ways of exercising psychic perceptivity and of testing it, can be confused in this way, by telepathy. Much of the work that has been done in the past *is* so confused. It is only of recent years that we have discovered how to eliminate telepathy of all kinds from our experiments. And the results so far have been very interesting.

The number of gifted psychics with sufficient confidence in their powers to co-operate in scientific experiments is extremely small, so the amount of work possible is limited.

The first thing is to realise that we have to start again from first principles. We have to try to find out whether there really are subtle planes of nature, subtle materials around us, which psychics can 'see'. This is the most fundamental part of our traditional teachings which we can hope to check. A study of the so-called etheric plane is most promising because this is supposed to be still physical and therefore objective in the ordinary sense of that term. Also, knowledge of the etheric—especially an ability to photograph it—could be of tremendous value to humanity in medical diagnosis.

No one is now likely to suggest doing what used to be done: that is, to test several psychics together to see if their observations agree. One might *expect* a telepathic linkage between psychics, anyhow.

It is said that some psychics can see a magnet glowing in the dark. One can readily make electro-magnets that can be switched on and off at random by a device in a box. The psychic can be asked to press a button every time the magnet is glowing. If she is consistently correct she will clock up a large score of correct statements on counters inside the box. If her etheric sight is merely unconscious dramatisation based on expectation—that is, if it is merely 'George' deceiving her and not giving her true information—then she will score about an equal number of right and wrong statements. As neither the psychic, nor anyone else, ever knows the state of the magnet at each trial (by use of one of the ordinary senses) telepathy is eliminated and the experiment will give a clear answer as to whether the psychic can or cannot obtain something consistent with this particular E.S.P. faculty.

Similar experiments are easy to devise which will test whether a psychic can or cannot see into a closed box when 'George' is prevented from getting information from the mind of the experimenter in charge. Telepathy of all kinds *must* be eliminated from the experiments. In the past it has not been, and the results are therefore inconclusive.

The same remarks apply to tests of the Delawarr 'black box'—the diagnostic instrument. Telepathy *must* be eliminated from experiments of that kind if they are to be meaningful. However, it is a sad fact that a great many psychic powers tend to dry up in a properly arranged scientific experiment.

This is a most unfortunate phenomenon and has been shown by Prof. J. B. Rhine of Duke University, North Carolina, to be due to the feeling relationship between the psychic and the research worker. If this relationship is completely harmonious, the results are sometimes good, *provided the psychic is not fatigued*. But if the arranger of the experiment is biased, over-critical or in any way out of friendly and harmonious rapport with the psychic, the experiment invariably fails.

We can now see why so many experiments in the past have not succeeded, although carried out with reputedly genuine psychics. Not only is it necessary to arrange such experiments in a manner which eliminates the possibility of telepathic communication, but everyone connected with the experiment *must be in a complete state of emotional harmony* with the psychic, and with one another. When this is so, the results are often strikingly successful.

2. SOME FUNDAMENTALS OF TELEPATHY

The last writer has mentioned various aspects of telepathy and some of the reasons for thinking it exists as a human faculty. In fact, more problems are likely to be raised if it does not exist than if it does. One might well think that all the work done in the past years should surely have settled beyond dispute a basic issue such as whether telepathy exists or not. In this respect, it is worth noting, that in the nature of things there are only two ways of knowing about something; by direct experience, and by reasoning of the mind.

Unfortunately, it is impossible to prove completely that anything is just as it may be imagined to be. It is only possible to prove conclusively that something is *not* as it was thought to be. This is a philosophical truism. Critics of telepathy have obviously not experienced telepathy; and if they refuse to accept other people's facts about it, there is no reasoning possible which can prove to them without a shadow of doubt that the faculty does exist. Only the ever mounting probability of it and the increasing difficulty of an alternative explanation of observed fact, will finally shift them over.

Detailed observations are steadily accumulating, and these tend to be more and more confusing without a sound framework in which to fit them. Accepting telepathy as a reasonable hypothesis, it is necessary to look at the fundametals in their most elementary form, in the attempt to discover in a logical way the principles that telepathy is likely to embody.

Cause and effect

Now the building of a hypothesis, or reasoned structure, can only be achieved if it is acknowledged that the rule of cause and effect applies throughout any plane of manifestation or level of consciousness which is considered. Much might be said on this one point for there are those even in the scientific world who support the idea that many of the actions in extra-sensory perception which are found so perplexing at present, are so because they are performed partly or wholly in a non-causal way. By this is meant, that cause may no longer imply an effect; that things may happen without a cause; that a state of randomness may exist. In such a crazy realm, sequence may be reversed; the effect of something may transpire before its cause, or an effect may appear for no particular reason at all. Now if this were truly possible, then plainly, there would be little point in our using our intellects to discover the laws of being; for if the facts of being do not follow the same rules as human reasoning, there is little hope of any reliable correspondence between them, except as a matter of good fortune.

As a start it is necessary, therefore, to frame a first postulate, namely, that the physical universe and any other associated planes of being or levels of consciousness, are ordered, and are subject to the laws of cause and effect.

This first postulate immediately rules out any theory of telepathy being due to mysterious and unknowable factors which suddenly produce an irrational result, and suggests instead that the functioning of telepathy and the rules that govern it will be found to fit precisely into the harmonious laws of man's nature.

Indirect and direct faculties

A second probable postulate is that there are intermediate states between physical existence and a related wholly non-manifested state of being, through which and in which energies of various kinds play and create cause and effect. If this postulate is accepted, an explanation of telepathic and clairsentient action is possible, namely that there are two basic types of faculty, each of which may be used on its own, according to the gifts of the person. First, the objective awareness of conditions by use of the intermediate states of being; one could call these states subtle bodies, though they may not actually be bodies as we think of them, but more in the nature of subtle energy counterparts. Secondly, the awareness directly between minds, of mental states or the results of mental activity.

In the intermediate states of being, the subtle bodies or counterparts are part of an energy continuum which inter-penetrates all matter as a matrix, and in which matter itself is only a localised condition. On this matrix all other energies have their specific impacts. Each physical form has its subtle counterparts within the main energy field and this field being a continuum, all individually energised portions of it are inter-linked so that dynamic changes can propagate.

In discussing this point, some have said: why should tele-pathy be propagated as if it were a wireless wave or light wave or shall we say, a thought wave? How do we know that consciousness at the telepathic level of working is not all one and that there is no need for *sending of thought impulses from anywhere to anywhere else*? No answer can yet be given to this question from the small amount of evidence that does seem to support the concept of intermediate states between pure non-manifested being and physical life as we know it. One can only suppose these states to be partly matter with some trend towards physical characteristics; they may have strange qualities, but presumably they will be bound by some of the basic principles of form and sequence. But do individuals transmit and receive to each other across their boundaries? Does each have a special 'wavelength' within a plenum of communication energy or are links established to convey a directly informing ebb and flow of consciousness? This is all wide open to conjecture at present.

Whatever the actual mode of communication by way of the postulated subtle bodies, the fact of telepathy is not re-cognised until it appears in the waking consciousness. In clairvoyance or clairaudience, perception is akin to physical sight and hearing in that the actual subtle sense signals have been reconstituted to make the information meaningful to the personal mind. This involves the process of interpretation into the sort of impressions which the mundane mind is accustomed to receiving from the physical senses. Such an interpretive process must always accompany perception through the subtle counterparts before any mental appreciation can follow. In the case of direct mind-to-mind action, the results are less liable to error because thoughts are received directly as thoughts and do not need interpretation.

Since, on this hypothesis, all physical forms have their subtle counterparts which link them to less material energy states, perception which involves neither the five physical senses, nor a direct thought to thought action, must involve the activity of these counterparts or bodies, followed by mental interpretation for the personal mind. Physical shapes, emotions, thoughts and spiritual influences will all be sensed at their levels and will be interpreted and classified in the waking consciousness. The main difference between the two modes of communication seems to be that whereas the first needs the sensing means of a subtle body followed by interpretation, the second can be achieved directly at its own level.

Precognitive telepathy

This bare hypothesis as to the *modus operandi* needs much detailed filling out from the results of further research, but even now it is possible to make certain inferences based on the postulates. An important one concerns the term and concept, precognitive telepathy. The idea behind the words is well known, it seeks to explain a certain class of phenomenon which defies analysis at present; people sometimes know things before they really should do according to all the laws of common sense; they know these things finally by a mental process and they know them precognitively; hence, precognitive telepathy, but for the sake of clarity, the logical derivation of this term should be considered.

Telepathy as herein described is a nearly instantaneous process if direct mind-to-mind action is concerned. In certain circumstances the rate of action of a complete telepathic process might be prolonged, if, for example, thought forms of a persistent nature can discharge themselves into another mind after a period of time; but the transfer of impressions can never be more rapid than instantaneous; the sensing of impressions within another mind can never, in any circumstances, give impressions to the senser which are not already there to be picked up at the moment of telepathic action. By a general causal hypothesis of precognition, it is possible to predict a future state by sensing both, the present state and the laws in operation to change that state. In this case the term precognitive telepathy means the sensing of a future state of another mind by the perception of the present state of that mind, and the laws in operation to change it. Should an act of precognising occur when all the factors relevant to the future state have not already been impressed on the mind being sensed, then this act is one of general precognition and not telepathic precognition at all. The future state in a determined situation is implicit in the present state and the laws in action. Thus precognitive telepathy can only foresee what is implicit at the moment of telepathic awareness; anything beyond this is precognition which has a much wider scope. Only in this rather restricted sense should the term precognitive telepathy be used.

Validity of hypothesis

In conclusion, it must be emphasised, that what has been said in hypothesis and its derived inferences will be valid only if the postulates are true. The basic assumptions of any reasoning set the form of the whole thought structure that follows, so if any of the conclusions appear unsatisfactory, then valid evidence that a postulate is not based on a true concept must be produced, or a fallacy demonstrated in the reasoning used. Successful challenge in either of these two aspects will suffice to make changes necessary, for in any subject of enquiry the theories that are formulated can only be as solid and confirmed as the known facts permit. Not nearly enough is known about telepathy; so for some time to come many differing viewpoints can be expected which will be neither corroborated nor logically disposed of.

3. THE PSYCHIC ASPECT OF TELEPATHY

As the result of a considerable amount of clairvoyant research during the last forty years or so, it is now realised how very little is known about psychical matters. Man has not yet discovered the laws which govern telepathy, and is always making the most elementary mistakes, because the whole question is involved with the emotional value which people give to it and their reactions to a cold impersonal criticism which they think may be hostile.

Theosophical literature in detail is increasingly open to doubt because of growing scientific knowledge, but this does not destroy its basic truth. One must be prepared to admit that some of the early works, to a very large extent, will not stand up to close examination in the light of present-day scientific knowledge.

Man lives in a world where telepathy is a constant and universal background to life. His capacity for 'tuning in' to the collective atmosphere around him is governed both by past psychological experience and by the E.S.P. he possesses. This is different in everyone. Any form of E.S.P. from the highest to the lowest, is channelled into physical consciousness along one of the avenues of the five senses. *Not enough significance is given to the image-making faculty of the mind, which works constantly*, and not much progress is likely to be made until there arises some form of scientific proof of the etheric field, as it is not recognised by ordinary science at the moment.

Man does not realise sufficiently the universality of telepathy. The world is not yet open to the idea that there is a world of mind in which all are manifesting, and that this implies mental or psychic interactions between everyone all the time. We are only aware of our own telepathic experiences very occasionally, when the etheric brain catches an invisible message and channels it into consciousness. We remain unaware that we are living every minute of our lives in a great ocean of thought forces.

In *The Web of the Universe*, E. L. Gardner likens the mental body of a human being to the disturbed water around a swimmer in the ocean. This agitated water is part of the ocean, and is really inseparable from it. Yet we succeed so well in enclosing it, i.e. in isolating our individual minds, that we now find telepathy surprising instead of inevitable.

Mystics in the past made reference to the possession of a 'special gift', by which they meant some form of extrasensory experience, but increasing knowledge is now taking the glamour out of psychism, and is bringing a realisation of the power that the ordinary person has within himself.

When taking part in group experiments a number of years ago, the chief clairvoyant had difficulty in obliterating the thoughts of other people around. Also in experimental E.S.P. the thoughts and the knowledge of scientists around interfered, and it was considered that most of the results of the older experiments were probably obtained by telepathy, not by communication or control by external entities.

However, man's real nature is at the spiritual level. The greatest experimental discovery that could be made would be of this reality and of the etheric bridge linking these higher realms of consciousness with the physical brain.

The material world is of a different order from the spiritual. It is limited by space and time, but also has something of the quality of the spiritual, changeless, timeless, Reality. From the material point of view it is a causal world giving rise to many complications, but from the spiritual point of view it is simple.

Two psychic experiences

During the summer of 1942 the writer participated in a series of experiments in telepathy with the late Dr. G. O. Atkinson of Dublin. The experiments were made fairly light-heartedly for our own private satisfaction and were not continuously recorded. From the beginning we got results well above chance, and after that we were chiefly interested in finding how we could improve our performance.

Our experiments were of two kinds. In one kind, one of us definitely attempted to send a message to the other, who endeavoured more or less passively to receive it. In the other kind, the sender more or less passively contemplated the message while the recipient took the more positive role and tried, as it were, to reach out and collect the message from him. Both sat in the same large room, usually ten to fifteen feet apart. The material of the 'messages' was provided by a pack of playing cards. We often found that the colour of the suit, black or red, was more easily transmitted and received than the number. Sometimes we included face cards, sometimes not. Sometimes we concentrated solely on numbers and ignored suits.

We learned a good deal from these experiments—about ourselves rather than about telepathy. Two experiences, however, made some impression at the time.

In the first case the writer was acting as the passive recipient, and Dr. Atkinson was endeavouring to send numbers, the numbers being determined by the card he drew from the pack in his hand. He drew a card, and then I saw the number shooting towards me with an explosive rapidity. The number, a 2, travelled or indeed shot through space as a figure about two-and-a-half to three feet high, but turned the wrong way round. When questioned as to just how he had tried to send his message, he said that he had simply looked at the recipient and imagined a large figure 2 super-imposed upon him. In effect, he created a 'thought form', and I saw its rear side or reverse, the obverse being of course towards him.

This experience was an interesting case of what would appear to be one person deliberately creating a 'thought form' and another person seeing it in the form in which it was created. There are, of course, other factors which are known to give rise to reverse or mirror images in experi-ments with the 'psi' factor; but in the present case this simple explanation seems reasonable and likely.

The second noteworthy experience occurred while Dr. Atkinson was at the far end of the room, turned sideways to me. He was to draw a card from the pack, hold it in his hand, in such a position that I could not see it, and to look at it quietly, while I tried to 'reach out' and discover what he was seeing. He drew a card accordingly and almost at once there was a feeling of a break-through, apparently inside my head, and I found myself looking for a brief instant through the sender's eyes and seeing his right hand holding a seven of hearts. It was noticeable that the odd pip, between the two vertical parallel lines of three pips down each side of the card, was at the top and not at the lower half of the card as he held it. What was seen in this way proved to be quite accurate, but we were not able to repeat this performance, and could find no reason why this little episode of 'clairvoyance' should occur on this particular occasion, nor could the machinery of it be explained.

The writer has had a good many experiences of the 'psi' factor in every-day life; but a shared experience, capable of clear and objective definition and mutual exchange of evidence between participants, is not very common. There was, of course, no evidence to offer to a third party in either of these incidents, and there is now only one survivor of those brief summer afternoon sessions when two people sat shutting their eyes or staring into space and exhorting each other to 'hot it up a little'. Yet these two incidents point to a field of experience upon which others may be interested to enter, and they certainly had value for those to whom they happened. A somewhat casual attitude and a lightly held notion of the result aimed at can provide opportunity for unexpected insights in connection with experiments of this nature.

M

Telepathic communication

In considering the method by which transference of thoughts from one person to another takes place one must be emancipated from the usual assumptions that apply to the transmission of information by means of waves in three-dimensional space, whether they be pressure waves, as in communication by sound, or transverse electro-magnetic waves. If any such emission occurred, capable of conveying thought, then it would almost certainly have been detected by now. Even if the brain did radiate for example, in a band of thermal frequencies, with wavelengths of a few microns, which it is not yet possible to detect and demodulate, then it would still be necessary to discover a mechanism by which thought impressions could be converted into wave form and not only transmitted, but also received and amplified.

In all forms of communication, by speech, writing, tele-graphy, touch, as in Braille, by visual signalling, either by semaphore, flashing lights, or hand movements, the content of the message must be reduced to a succession of coded symbols, or impulses of specific intensity or duration. This code must then be translated back into the receiving message at the receiving end. The message is therefore unintelligible without this coding and decoding function which occurs at either end. The same conditions might also apply to tele-pathy, irrespective of the fact that the message is not con-veyed through intervening distance in a way which we understand at present. One might have to assign a common code for the sender and receiver, most suitable for the medium in which the information is to be carried. Telepathy may therefore be a special skill, like that of a wireless operator, which anyone can acquire with sufficient training.

Apparent irrationality of telepathy

In dealing with telepathic communication certain bizarre conditions are met which ought to be included in the 'field theory' of this phenomenon: (a) The amplitude of the received impression is unaffected by distance. (b) There is no absolute time dependence, i.e. the impression may be received *before* it is sent, or varying periods of time afterwards, not related to distance. (c) Complete pictures, words, feelings, are received without any evidence of being built up, as would be necessary if the information were being transmitted in a series of coded impulses, as with a wire picture, which is transmitted line by line. (d) Telepathic communication may be involuntary, it can even occur in the form of dreams, divorced from intelligent control.

The above conditions, and many others relating to telepathy, seem so foreign to rational scientific ideas that it is not strange that the examination of them should be classed as metaphysics. In fact all the conditions which have been specified, 'Lack of time dependence', 'lack of intelligent control', etc., seem to suggest a connection with the unconscious mind.

Freud intimates that the unconscious has no conception of time, that ideas and impressions from different ages are telescoped together. He says that the unconscious has no relation to outer reality. When there is a wish for something to happen it simply happens. In the unconscious there is no doubt, no uncertainty, everything is absolute—it is only the censorship emanating from the higher conscious system that modifies this condition of absoluteness.

The general view of the unconscious mind is that it consists of the buried and fused impressions of the whole prehistory of humanity, even of living things themselves. People who have taken drugs like Mescalin and obtained rapport with their unconscious sometimes speak of going back through the whole process of evolution of life, from the mineral, through the vegetable to the animal. There thus seems to be a common bond of experience which links us all through the pathway of the unconscious, an etheric short-cut perhaps which exists in this immense storehouse of shared impressions, a region of contact for the astral sense of touch, if one regresses to a suitable point in time.

A picture of the unconscious can be conveyed by describing it as a path through a forest. The trees on each side represent events which are related to the unconscious in time. The conscious mind might be like a man walking along the path; this motion represents his passage through time, meeting the various events symbolised by the trees. This man will occasionally have glimpses through the trees of other paths running in the same direction through the forest, with people walking on them, keeping abreast of him—such glimpses might be compared to involuntary telepathy. His unconscious, however, is the whole route the path takes, stretching into the past behind and the future ahead. By using this path the individual can reach along it to some point where telepathic contact is possible, through the medium of a common experience, or in analogy, where someone can be glimpsed through the forest.

Telepathy probably an unconscious function

If one accepts this idea that telepathy is an unconscious function, then it is necessary to discover the means of translating a message reliably into a form suitable for transmission and reception. It might be reasonable to assume that the 'code' would be something that served to stimulate mental concentration, or the memory faculty. Could it be a system of drawing material rapidly from the unconscious into the conscious mind which was under the control of the individual, so that each fact appeared in its correct sequence? Such memorising systems (mnemonic systems) have been known from very early times.

The Visual-Symbol system was devised around the year 500 B.C. by the Greek poet Simonides. According to Cicero this system occurred to Simonides under dramatic circumstances. At a banquet he was invited to provide a recitation as part of the entertainment. Almost immediately after delivering his recitation Simonides was called away and had scarcely left the house when the floor of the banquet room collapsed, killing the host and all his guests. Naturally the relatives wished to sort out the bodies, but these were so mutilated as to be unrecognisable. However, Simonides had observed during his recital the position occupied by each person in the room, and by searching the wreckage in the appropriate places was able to identify the bodies. He could recall who was present by remembering where they were. This incident set Simonides thinking, if such was the case with places and people surely names, objects and even ideas could be better memorised by assigning them fixed positions in space. He would imagine, as vividly and with as much detail as possible, a room. Each item he wished to commit to memory he would visualise as being in a certain part of that room. Then when he wanted to recall these items he would systematically explore the room and find each item located in a particular position.

In the mid-nineteenth century a man from Cambridge, Henry Herdson, developed a system which dispensed with the locality of the visual symbols and instead assigned to them a numerical sequence, which served the same purpose of bringing them forward from the subconscious in the correct order. His first symbol might be a candle, or something elongated like a figure one, then a swan, which looks like a figure two; next a trident with its three prongs, and so on. One could select a sequence of objects in this way for numbers even up to a hundred.

The next step was to visualise the information one wished to memorise alongside the symbol one had assigned to the number. Say for example one wished to memorise the cities of the world in the correct order of their size—such as Tokyo, London, New York, etc. One might picture Tokyo as a candle around which people are clustering; London as a flock of swans on the Thames; New York as the bootblack with a three-legged stool, according to the order one assigned. Each object is visualised as concretely as possible, with distinct individual features. Further, this pairing of the city and the object is not just a juxaposition, the two things are brought into a definite relation with each other and *the more ridiculous, far-fetched and striking this relationship is, the easier it is to remember it*. With practice it becomes possible to visualise two objects and to bring them together in a lively and dramatic way; then these two can be dismissed from the memory and the next pair visualised.

Such mnemonic systems could be considered to have some

relationship to the transmission of thought. Conscious effort is necessary to assemble a message in topographical form or in relation to preconceived archetypes in the memory. The act of making these arrangements could result in an impression being transmitted. It is reasonable to suppose that the power with which a message is sent out depends upon the attention given to the particular thought.

The author's own experience can reinforce this contention. When away from home he bought his wife two presents, a stole and a necklace. His wife received the telepathic message that he had bought the former article but not the latter one. It should be pointed out that the stole cost four times as much and made an appreciable dent in his purse. It is reasonable to suppose he gave the more costly purchase more thought than the cheaper one. Not only this, for the colour of the stole had to be decided, and he had to picture his wife wearing it with a number of dresses. This was his code for linking the idea telepathically, and inadvertently the idea was transmitted to her.

Technique of telepathic transmission

It seems reasonable to suppose that this method of coding the proposed message consists therefore of transposing its successive elements, piece by piece, into juxtaposition with some form of personal experience, so as to spread it along the pathway of the unconscious. If this idea is correct, then it is easier for people who have a common bond of experience to communicate with each other, i.e. relatives or man and wife. They do this simply by putting the message into a relationship with some experience that happened to them together. But since, as already mentioned, the whole of humanity has to

a certain extent common archetypes of evolutionary experience, circumstances of life, religious beliefs, then it is
possible that telepathy on a much wider scale is feasible. In
the ordered world of the scientist there is also a common
language of physics, chemistry, electronics, etc., which has
the same possibilities.

It also appears that the transmission of thought is on dia-
metrically opposite lines to that of an electro-magnetic
wave, as defined by Maxwell's equations. In the case of the
electro-magnetic wave the efficiency of transmission depends upon the flux or variation of energy through spatial
co-ordinates. In transmitting thought, however, spatial
co-ordinates are of no real consequence, and instead of flux,
or sudden change, one should hold the thought steadily in
one's attention, at the very most travelling gently from one
association to the next after allowing time for it to sink in.
This again suggests that the medium of transmission is not
the capacitive and inductive extensions of space but instead
a system of invariant archetypes, absolute conceptions,
which the attention lights up as if they were so many
beacons.

What of the reception of messages? In his book, *The
Mind and its Mechanism*, Bousfield suggests that sleep creates
favourable conditions for telepathic reception. He adds that
the message may arrive simultaneously with the transmission, but due to the complicated process of translation
through the unconscious it might only penetrate to the
conscious mind during sleep the following night. This
helps to account for the lack of correspondence between an
event and a presentiment in time. Similarly, a person who
received a message during sleep might, on waking, believe
he had received the message the previous day, before it was

actually sent. Recollection can play strange tricks if one is not careful to record the precise moment of an impression being received.

For accuracy the mind of the receiver should be a complete blank, a clean slate. If one tries this for a second or two the difficulty becomes apparent. Only a person practised in meditation would be likely to succeed. Consciousness abhors a vacuum. The quality of mental concentration necessary for this purpose is so rare that telepathic 'receivers' are hard to find, although everyone has a trace of the ability. Under hypnosis the condition of a blank mind is also produced and therefore telepathic reception is possible in this state for some people who could not achieve it otherwise. Day-dreaming can also be fertile ground for the implantation of telepathic impressions. While on this point it might be mentioned that Freud himself believed in the possibility of telepathy occurring in dreams and in involuntary statements made during analysis by free association. He mentions examples in *New Lectures on Psycho-Analysis*. Freud's interpretation is important because it shows how dreams received telepathically can be distorted by the subconscious desires of the recipient. In a disturbed and emotional state telepathy might be impossible, and the work of psycho-analysis in serving to bring supressed desires to the surface of consciousness may be a valuable preliminary to an attempt at communication.

Speaking generally, the reception of a message implies a measure of amplification, in that a small signal may be converted into a larger physical change. Everyone is familiar with the method of recall known as Reintegration, which consists of keeping mementos to bring back certain things to mind. Tying knots in one's handkerchief, for instance, may help to recall a situation which existed at the time the knot was tied, which in turn leads to the remembering of an engagement. Thus a tiny part of the experience produces a disproportionate effect, the recall of much more material than one would expect from so slight a cause. This can be used as the analogy for psychic amplification which occurs in the mind of a person sensitive to telepathic impressions. The important thing to be noted, however, is that the amplification cannot occur *unless the event, of which the impression is a part, has actually been experienced by the recipient.*

The whole process of telepathy may thus be summarised in the following manner:—

Transmission: the association of abstract material in juxtaposition with facets of an actual, shared experience, involving mental concentration.

Reception: reintegration of mementos into the full context of a shared experience, with a subsequent interpretation of the associated abstract material.

The method of transmission described in preceding paragraphs must be different for persons who have no capacity for visual imagery. In mnemonic exercises they would have most success when the association is given in verbal terms some catch phrase which links a string of facts together. For example, the notes of the lines on sheet music E, G, B, D, F can be linked in the phrase 'every good boy deserves favour' and the spaces between the lines F, A, C, E again make a word.

Verbalists would also find the Digit-Letter system of a German, Stanislau Winckelmann, first published in 1684, easier to get on with. This system is especially designed to assist in the memorisation of digit sequences, like dates, or quantities. Each digit is symbolised by a letter, or letters of the alphabet; these letters are then built up into easily remembered phrases.

In telepathic transmission the associations would not be with remembered scenes, but with things heard—songs, verse, extracts from plays and so on. Reintegration would be effected by a few notes, or a word to give the whole context. Most success would be obtained where the phrase had some lively, striking or amusing construction.

Objective tests of telepathy

It seems fairly evident, for many reasons which are well known, that in successful telepathy experiments two minds have a relationship to one another which is almost completely at the unconscious (or sub-liminal) level, i.e. below the threshold of consciousness. In fact some go so far as to say that everyone is psychic, that we all receive telepathic impressions from other people, both the living and the so-called dead, but that most of us have not discovered the technique for rendering such impressions overt (even to ourselves). In this view we can all, for example, 'divine' water or other substances, this faculty being a capacity of the greater part of us which is outside the normal waking consciousness, but we have not yet learned how to cause the information to move a divining rod or pendulum, or to operate the diagnostic instrument in radiesthesia.

But perhaps other more subtle physiological changes take place when we are in telepathic rapport with someone else, or when we consciously wonder about the presence of water in the ground beneath our feet, or of disease in the body of a patient whose blood spot we have. If such physiological changes do take place, and if they could be detected, then these would be facts of very great importance and might indicate the way to a major advance in this subject.

These are some thoughts which occurred to the writer when he read in the *Journal of the Society for Psychical Research*, December 1959, a paper by Stepan Figar, M.D., entitled, 'The Application of Plethysmography to the Objective Study of So-called Extrasensory Perception'. This paper describes experiments in which the author recorded by means of a mechanically-operated pen recorder changes in the volume of the left hand and the distal part of the forearm of a subject, these parts being inserted into the cylinder of a mechanical water plethysmograph, i.e. a water-filled space into which the hand could be inserted from outside by means of a sealed flexible glove, changes in the water level moving the pen of the recorder. Dr. Figar states that such volume changes are an expression of the behaviour of the peripheral blood vessels, diminution in volume being generally interpreted as vaso-constriction and increase as vaso-dilation. The vascular reaction, like most autonomic reactions, is not under normal conditions subject to voluntary control.

The first subject was comfortably seated in an easy chair in semi-darkness, his left hand being arranged as described, and the equipment started. When the tracing (plethysmogram) showed the 'at rest' condition a piece of mental arithmetic was presented to the subject by the experimenter, i.e. he was asked to multiply two two-digit numbers. The mental effort resulted (as is well known) in a vascular reaction, and the plethysmogram at this point showed a significant lowering. (Such vasoconstrictive reactions normally accompany any kind of mental effort). After the effort a re-establishment of the 'at rest' condition followed. These mental efforts were repeated at irregular intervals.

A second subject was seated in exactly the same way during the experiment just described, one of his hands being similarly arranged. The second subject was seated at the other side of a thick curtain and it was impossible for him to receive any kind of auditory or other signal from the first subject or the experimenter, who were invisible to him. The tracing relative to his hand was arranged to appear on the same roll of paper as that for the first subject, a tube being brought through the curtain to the drum. No information was given to the subjects as to the nature of the experiments and the purpose of these remained completely unknown to them.

Altogether 119 experiments were carried out with 32 people (16 couples) arbitrarily selected. In 44 of these experiments there occurred in the second subject (the 'percipient') a vaso-constrictive reaction (lowering of the plethysmographic curve) during the period in which the first subject (the 'agent') was engaged in the mental arithmetic. The lowering of the curve for the second subject began 2 to 10 seconds after the beginning of the mental effort of the first, i.e. while *one* of the subjects was calculating there occurred a significant lowering in *both* plethysmographic curves. In 75 cases no vaso-constrictive or other reactions occurred in the second subject while the first was making a calculation, i.e. only the curve for the latter showed a lowering.

In some parts of the records it was noted that parallelism between the so-called spontaneous vascular reactions lasted for up to 10 minutes, giving the impression of some kind of synchronisation between the two plethysmograms. (A mother and son as 'agent' and 'percipient' showed a particularly striking parallelism.) Such parallel phases appeared in the records of only some pairs of subjects and even then only for a time.

At the end of an experiment the subject who had not engaged in calculation was asked whether he had noticed any special feelings or impressions. Their reports were uniformly negative. They often in fact became fully or partially asleep and it was in such a state that a greater amount of positive reaction was observed.

The author points out the relatively small number of experiments made and the need for caution in evaluating the results. He mentions particularly possible other factors such as changes in breathing which might have been picked up by the 'percipient', even though the steady humming of the electric motor driving the drum was intended to submerge and exclude them.

The author refers to other experiments in telepathic phenomena in which other autonomic reactions have been recorded, and recommends the application of physiological and graphical methods of research, e.g. cardiotachography, pneumography, recording of the electrical state of the skin, etc. Such results might be of great importance in relation to the general question of the existence and nature of so-called extra-sensory perception.

In the same *Journal* Dr. D. J. West comments on Dr. Figar's paper and points out, from a tabulation of the deflections occurring in the plethsymograms of the two subjects over 1,646 10-second intervals recorded, observed coincidences of five times the chance expectation in the resting periods, and two and a half times the chance expectation in the periods of mental arithmetic concentration. Such large deviations from chance are rare in E.S.P. experiments and Dr. West suggests that Dr. Figar's technique could prove an enormous advance. It is important to note that the most impressive number of coincidences occurs during the rest periods, suggesting that *the presentation of stimulation to the 'agent' plays no part in the synchronisation of deflections, which occurs as well, if not better, by the mere fact of the two subjects* sitting down on either side of a screen, near each other.

The writer suggests that work of this kind is well worth further research. Evidently the next stage would be to increase the distance between the two subjects, which would necessitate electrical means of transmitting the physiological changes, and perhaps try other autonomic reactions also.

Radiesthesia

N

An experiment in radiesthesia

Radiesthetic practitioners claim to be able (*a*) to diagnose and (*b*) to treat disease in a distant patient, by using a specimen of blood or saliva on a piece of white filter paper, which they put into a 'diagnostic instrument'. This instrument consists of an 'electronic box' containing various wires, magnets and dials, and a cell in which to place the specimen to be diagnosed, but bears no relation to any scientific instrument that a qualified scientist or electrical engineer could recognise. Mr. De la Warr, the main manufacturer of these boxes in this country, admitted in an action heard in the High Court in 1960 that he did not know how the 'box' worked, though he honestly believed in its efficacy. Having placed the specimen from the patient in the cell in the box, a number of mental questions are asked designed to elicit the information required. At the same time, a strip of rubber, also on the instrument, is stroked with a finger. It is believed by the practitioner that if a positive answer is appropriate the finger 'sticks' to the rubber. By a skilful asking of the right questions, all the diseases from which the patient is suffering (or perhaps going to suffer from) are determined. The diagnosis contains a large number of items, some few of which ever correspond to clinically recognisable diseases. But, on the other hand, many other reactions are said to be present, and to refer to specific conditions—e.g. of the endocrine glands, etc.—which, however, are not clinically evident even by the subtlest of tests.

It was felt that, in view of the claims, it would be useful if some tests were made, and it appeared that as a first attempt it should prove easy for blood specimens, taken at the same time from any one person, to have sufficient consistently recognisable reactions for them to be distinguished from others. (For the moment the matter of successful treatment was left aside; it is almost impossible to find any practitioner able to give case records which would satisfy an entirely objective assessor: but this does not mean they do not exist.) Hence this preliminary experiment was undertaken, fully realising that the material provided was not enough for statistical evaluation. On the other hand, if the claims of radiesthetic workers were valid, there should be a high preponderance of success even in so small-scale an experiment.

It was thought expedient to work in such a way that telepathy, the workings of which are exceedingly insidious, should be made as unlikely as possible. Hence Dr. X. was asked to provide eight specimens of blood, taken from four different people. These were of both sexes, and some were recognisably ill, some were not. He put the small pieces of blotting-paper (handled only with forceps) in small envelopes, and the latter into large ones. They were all double indexed so that no one person would be able to recognise any of them. They were mixed, and one specimen removed at random. The remainder, consisting of three pairs and an odd one, were then sent successively to two experienced radiesthesists who were asked to pick out the pairs, and decide which was the odd one.

The results were: *Operator A* picked out the odd specimen and paired one set of bloods correctly, being wrong in two. *Operator B* picked out the single specimen, but was wrong in each of the three pairs.

This experiment failed to show results which could not be

attributed to chance. But one might make the following comments:

1. A single such experiment on so small a scale is by no means conclusive. Indeed, many more are needed to get at the real facts.

2. It may be that other operators (the two who did the experiment accepted it as reasonable) of radiesthetic apparatus may think the test was too difficult, or in some way unfair, but since radiesthesists usually give an enormous amount of detail about their patients, one would have expected 100% correct answers in such a very simple experiment.

Some difficulties of radiesthesia diagnosis

The practice of radiesthesia falls into two distinct sections, diagnosis and treatment, and mainly the former is considered here. The claim is made by radiesthesists that they can diagnose in detail the disease from which a person is suffering, by examining a spot of blood or other specimen which has come from the patient. The specimen is usually examined in conjunction with a special apparatus which enables the operator to intensify, and clarify, the details of the diagnosis. This enables him to avoid making vague, general statements, and to describe categorically which organs, or parts of organs, are in a state of ill health. It is found in regard to the apparatus, that only people with a certain type of E.S.P. can make use of it. In the hands of other people it is useless. This has modified the view, at one time widely held, that the apparatus itself had special diagnostic properties and it is now generally recognised that the whole key to radiesthetic diagnosis is to be found in the operator himself.

When the phenomenon of radiesthesia is in operation we therefore have three essential factors. (1) A special type of operator, (2) the instrument used, and (3) the patient who supplies the specimen. Since the first two are unknown quantities, it is essential, if we are to investigate these three factors, that in order to avoid a third unknown, the patient's illness be well-defined, and accurately diagnosed before starting simple test experiments. Such diagnosis must be capable of being checked by independent laboratory tests made by any competent person trained in medical diagnosis, and must not depend on someone's opinion. Moreover, steps must be taken, by double indexing, to prevent the radiesthesist from knowing anything of the origin of the specimen, and hence the correct diagnosis, until after he has finished his experiment. It has been found that when careful experiments have been done in this way, the operator has very rarely been able to give a correct diagnosis. Some have failed consistently. Others have been right at times and wrong at others. This rather suggests there are at least two categories of radiesthesists—those who *always* fail under test conditions, and those who *sometimes* fail. The first group can be put on one side as honestly believing they can diagnose, when in actual fact they can not. The second group, however, raises subtle problems as to the cause of their intermittancy.

Now it is a well known phenomenon that the power of any form of E.S.P. tends to diminish quickly as the person exercising it gets tired, and this probably explains quite a number of the failures in the second group. But one wonders why in the first group, the ability to diagnose disease often *seemed* to be demonstrated, and yet on careful examination was found to be illusory. One suspected that perhaps there were different types of radiesthetic ability, but not all of them were suitable for diagnosing from a blood spot, and on further investigation this proved to be the case. This interesting discovery explains many of the anomalies of radiesthesia, and why so many contradictory statements have been made in its connection.

So far, at least five different types of radiesthesia have been discovered:—

Type 1. This is a true psychometric type of E.S.P. in which the operator receives from the blood spot subtle vibrations which originated in the patient, and some of these are therefore of the same nature as those produced by the ailment. These affect the consciousness of the operator, and by means of the apparatus he uses, he is able to interpret them in the form of a detailed and accurate diagnosis.

Type 2. In this group, whatever is *believed* about the patient by the waking consciousness of the operator, will be recorded by his apparatus, whether his belief be accurate, inaccurate, prejudiced or due to fantasy. Full details will be enumerated, giving a superficial appearance of a correct diagnosis, but will always be only details of what the operator himself *thinks* to be the case. The diagnosis will therefore at times be correct. This unfortunately leads to a false sense of ability on the part of the operator, in spite of the fact that this 'conscious opinion' type of radiesthesia, by its very nature, is useless for diagnostic purposes.

Type 3. This is an extremely rare form of radiesthesia, in which an unexposed photographic plate is put into one compartment of the apparatus used, and a blood spot in another. The plate is then developed, and often shows a photograph of some part of the body which is said to be that part of the patient which is diseased.

In a long series of experiments an apparently true relation was sometimes found between the photograph and the ailment. At other times there was failure, and after numerous experiments it was discovered that a successful image only appeared if a certain member of the operating team happened to touch the unexposed plate at some time prior to its development. In some way his physical touch imparted an extra sensitivity to the plate, enabling it to record an image while still wrapped in its opaque covering.

As an E.S.P. phenomenon this seems to be unique, and is naturally of intense interest, but when we consider its usefulness for accurate diagnosis of illness, many doubts arise. First, the image is usually rather vague and of a general nature, indicating a whole organ, for example, rather than giving details of what part of the organ is affected, and of its serious or simple nature.

Secondly, one needs to know the source of such an image. If it is due to a thought-form that the extra-sensitive plate has been able to photograph, one needs to know who created that thought-form. Was it the patient or one of the operators? If any of these produced it, it is again useless for diagnostic purposes, as it is not a photograph of the actual organ, but represents the thought created by someone's imagination. That the latter is probably the correct explanation is strongly suggested by the fact that the Mr. X. at the De la Warr Laboratories who was always connected with successful photographs of this kind, said he could not produce satisfactory images on the unexposed plate unless he knew beforehand the nature of the patient's illness. Much work needs to be done in order to find how exactly these images are produced.

Type 4. Conscious telepathy from one person to another is now an established fact, and certain people in this group find they can make telepathic contact with a patient by using his blood spot as a means of rapport. Having thus tuned in, as it were, to the patient's mind, they are able to record through their radiesthesia instrument a description of what they find in that patient's mind concerning his illness. Many

true facts about the illness may thus be recorded, but as once
again the operator is not contacting the actual disease, he can
only receive details of what the patient *thinks* about himself.
This, as every doctor knows, is almost always inaccurate,
and depends on many variable factors not directly connected
with the illness. For instance, a patient may have thought
for years he had heart disease, because his mother told him
that as a baby he had a weak heart. Yet in actual fact he may
have had a sound heart for most of his life, but being convinced otherwise, anyone in telepathic rapport with him
would receive powerful thoughts of heart disease.

Type 5. To make the subject still more complex and unsatisfactory as a means of diagnosis, we find those belonging
to this group have more than one type of radiesthetic E.S.P.
combining, say, Type 1 with Type 2. Moreover, these two
methods of approach may vary from day to day in their
dominance, so that on one occasion the operator finds he is
exercising his psychometric powers as in Type 1 and getting
a certain number of correct diagnoses, whereas on another
occasion this power may be in abeyance and only the
'Conscious Opinion' variety be functioning, with its complete lack of usefulness as a means of diagnosis.

On considering these five types of radiesthesia:

1. psychometry,
2. conscious opinion,
3. touch and photograph,
4. telepathy to patient's mind,
5. combination of two types,

the last four are completely unreliable as a means of diagnosis, while the first is only correct at times, and it is

impossible to tell when that may be. We are thus driven to the conclusion that while the phenomenon of radiesthesia is of great interest academically, it is quite unable to take the place of, or equal, normal methods of diagnosis.

To touch briefly on the other section of this subject that deals with treatment, it has already been shown by the Medical Research Group of the T.R.C. in *The Mystery of Healing*, 1958, that any benefit radiated to a patient at a distance does not come from the machine used, but from the operator himself.

Throughout history it has been known that if anybody repeatedly sends out definite thoughts of health, harmony, courage, and optimism to a patient, the latter will benefit if he is receptive. All that is needed is a knowledge of thought control, a sympathetic nature, and a clear determination to help if possible. This method of helping the sick is practised widely in all countries, both by individuals and groups, and in the aggregate must have an enormous effect in lessening some of the suffering of the world, but no mechanical apparatus is necessary, nor any powers of E.S.P., for its success.

Pendulum and radiesthesia

For a number of months a thorough investigation was made by a member of the Theosophical Society into diagnosis by means of a pendulum, and the whole atmosphere was found to be full of the glamour, illusion and deception of the usual kind associated with psychic practices; moreover pendulum users and practitioners were found to be very disinclined to submit their work to proper testing.

The pendulums or radiesthetic machines were found to tell one *nothing* of themselves. All depended on the sensitivity of the operator, and his intuition and knowledge of the body and its diseases.

Two of the tests will speak for themselves.

The interest of a group of people in a hotel was aroused by telling them that the pendulum would swing in a straight line over the male hand and in a circle over the female hand. They happily found this correct.

Later another group was contacted (neither group knowing anything of the subject) and told the *exact opposite*, viz. that the pendulum would swing in a circle over a male hand and in a straight line over a female hand. They too happily found this to be so.

In order to defeat the memory of the operator (which is very important in this experiment) 15–20 children's signatures were obtained from a private school. These were carefully diagnosed with the pendulum for certain characteristics, and recorded, then the list was put away for three months. Again making the diagnosis they were compared with the previous ones, and it was found that the two sets of readings could not have been much more different!

An interesting test would be to have arranged two equal sets of vegetables, say, tomato, cucumber, lettuce, carrot, onion, beet, celery—one arranged under a cloth without the knowledge of the operator. The latter could then 'pick up' the vibration of a vegetable and try to find its position under the cloth. To a practitioner, an offer was made to arrange a test with small medicine bottles, some with homeopathic remedies in them, some without, under a cloth for him to distinguish between them with his pendulum. He refused.

It was found that by holding a pendulum as still as possible one could *think* it to any degree on a scale and it would gradually swing there without any *conscious* muscular direction on the part of the operator.

It is obvious that the utmost alertness and a scientific attitude is necessary, and that good and earnest people may be easily enmeshed in self-deception.

Comments on Radiesthesia

The writer has been in touch with radiesthesia, etc., ever since 1923, in the early days when Abram's method was introduced into this country by Dr. Mather Thomson, with whom the writer worked. The following comments may therefore be of some use.

First, it should be realised that Abram's theories derive simply on his own findings, and have never been scientifically substantiated. This may also be said to apply to practically every subsequent development of the methods. 'Rates' and 'wavelength' are based on the work of individuals, using all kinds of apparatus from the very simplest to highly complicated ones. The simplest work just as well as the others. Hence, these 'rates' must be looked upon as a convenient convention and not as representing actual energy-'wavelength'.

Secondly, it must be recognised that the apparatus works just as well, both for treatment and diagnosis, whether it is intact and properly connected, or not, *provided the operator thinks it is suitable*. This applies to every machine so far devised, including the De la Warr–Corte camera. (See *Light*, March 1957, article by Landau and Firebrace which has upset a great deal of theory about apparatus and cameras.) This throws the whole matter back on to the principle which has long been felt to be at work; that the process depend on the 'psychism' of the operator, using some focus (hazel twig, pendulum, De la Warr apparatus, etc.) much as a fortune-teller uses cards, tea-leaves or a crystal. This is not being insulting; there is no doubt that radiesthesia works sometimes. The main bone of contention with practitioners is that they so often diagnose all kinds of diseases for which there is not the slightest justification on any grounds whatever, then proceed to 'cure' them. The apparatus is a focus which is necessary to the operator, and hence, as justifiably used as a gardener uses a spade or pick, to do what he cannot do unaided. If this is realised, it simplifies the whole matter considerably.

Before the theories put forward can be accepted, they need scientific justification and confirmation; and of course, the concept of the psychic element in both diagnosis and treatment makes this difficult. On the other hand, the concept of etheric and vital fields helps by providing a theoretical background, in which the phenomena of radiesthesia are more understandable than on a crudely physical basis.

On the matter of treatment, too, the mental or psychic element is most important. In fact, starting from the philosophical viewpoint elaborated in Raynor Johnson's *Nurslings of Immortality*, a certain person is already obtaining results in 'treating' half a field (the other half being used as a control) purely by *mental* focusing, and it would seem that any results are 'telepathic', i.e. depend on the mental, not the physical, levels for the effects. Moreover, nowhere yet has the writer been able to obtain satisfactory clinical evidence of disease being cured by distant radiesthesia. In every case looked into, either there are no records, or they are so indefinite as to frustrate any real assessment of what has happened.

Human consciousness and its phenomena

The three divisions of human consciousness

The word 'consciousness' conveys different meanings to different people.

To most of us our waking consciousness seems to be just a simple state of awareness, but on examination is found to consist of three main divisions, each division having special characteristics of its own not shared by the others, as well as certain features in common.

Instinctive motivation

During the long time consciousness evolved in the animal kingdom, it was continuously goaded into new activities by external stimuli, and by constantly adjusting itself to these changing conditions, developed an automatic system of extraordinary complexity and perfection. However, this wakeful awareness, in which the animal always did what was best for itself in every changing circumstance, was not *self*-conscious, but instinctive. It ate, or slept, or took exercise, or indulged in other activities, only when necessary, and always in correct amounts. It never did these things by reasoning, but always automatically, according to its *feelings*.

Logical reasoning

Then Man came, bringing with him a *self-conscious* mind, with reasoning ability, imagination, and powers of anticipation, all of which were added to the instinctive wisdom of his animal ancestors. But having no self-conscious past experience, he was devoid of any system of values on which to base his thought, and could only experiment with his mind by observing and reasoning on what he saw, or experienced through his other senses.

In spite of this ability to reason logically about his sense impressions, his conclusions were often far from the truth since his feelings were frequently misinterpreted, and he also found it difficult to distinguish between instinctive impulses and original thought.

This great limitation of the human mind still remains, for though a system of logic may in itself be sound, it will not lead to the truth unless its premises are true. If they are false, it becomes 'an organised way of going wrong with confidence'!

As time passed, man's factual mind discovered that certain things and ideas could be grouped together because of attributes they had in common, so gradually fundamental principles were recognised as standing in their own right without being part of a system of logic. This ability to deal with abstract principles was a new step in the approach to truth, bringing richness and greater comprehension to the mind. And this is the instrument of consciousness used by the majority of mankind today: a self-conscious mind, with its concrete and abstract sections constantly modified by primitive desires and feelings which it tends to rationalise.

It follows, so far, that all man's knowledge has been acquired through his five senses by external observation, and is thus found to be fragmentary, and often misleading.

Illumined consciousness

As the race has advanced, however, it has been noticed that from time to time many people get flashes of illumination on

o

various problems that are not the result of rational thought. It is as if one had peeped into Nature's Answer Book and saved oneself the trouble of a prolonged chain of reasoning.

Some of these cases can be explained by the action of one's abstract mind summarising a number of factors, correlating them with accumulated knowledge from the past, and presenting the resulting solution to the waking consciousness.

When this happens, the answer is often right, but sometimes it is only partly so, and at others it may ultimately be proved to be wrong, the reason being that the proportion of truth contained in a summary is dependent on the accuracy of the original observations stored up in the mind. If these were faulty, then the summary and correlation done by the mind will lack truth in the same proportion as in the original observations.

But other cases are not so easily explained, for if we take the outstanding instances of history when completely new and revolutionary concepts have suddenly appeared in someone's mind, presenting aspects of truth never known before and bringing about great changes in the outlook of humanity, and add them to the lesser and more common degrees of non-logical illumination with which many people are acquainted from time to time, we are forced to recognise a new type of consciousness beginning to emerge.

This illumined consciousness seems to work by a process of expansion which *involves* the idea or thing contemplated, and so gets to know it at first hand from *within*, and not from external observation through the senses. For this reason, it always carries with it a sense of certainty, and subsequent events will not prove it to be erroneous as may happen in the mental summary cases, for the latter are ultimately dependent on sense observations which may be inaccurate whereas the former depends on a conscious unity with the object considered.

This latter type of consciousness which is slowly developing in the human race has often been called Intuition, but as the latter has been used to include the mental summary type of approach to truth, as well as the more accurate unifying type of consciousness, it would probably be better to use the term Illumined Consciousness to specify the latter, and restrict its use to that type of consciousness only.

There are also certain 'hunches' of a lesser nature that must not be confused with either of the foregoing, such as when one has an overwhelming feeling one is going to meet a certain person, and then does so. This is usually a simple case of telepathy. The still more ordinary type of 'hunch' one gets that a certain horse is going to win a race is usually a pure guess, and when successful, a coincidence!

To recapitulate briefly, man's self-consciousness can be seen as working through his mind in three different ways.

1. Most commonly his mind is activated simply by his instinctive feelings and desires, which stimulate him into building up a way of life in which they are the chief architects. Occasionally members of this group use the mind for original thought, but such cases are not very common.

2. The second group is the mainly mental type and is motivated by ideas rather than feelings. It appears in two varieties: (a) where cold logical reasoning and factual thinking, as in High Court Judges and mathematicians, are the main activities of consciousness; (b) a more comprehensive mental type which has good reasoning power and is also able to appreciate general principles and abstract ideas.

3. In the third group the Illumined Consciousness is being born. When this is functioning it brings greater insight into the truths of Nature, sometimes in small ways, and occasionally in brilliant flashes, influencing the finer reaches of the abstract section of the mind, and bringing a knowledge of reality which cannot be experienced in any other way. Such knowledge brings with it the imprint of truth, and although subsequent discovery may enhance and expand it, it will not prove it wrong.

The accompanying diagram expresses these ideas concisely.

1. *Instinctive Consciousness* + *Concrete Mind* → Common everyday mind.
   (desires and feelings)

2. *Pure Mental Consciousness* (a) Coldly logical and concrete → Factual mind.
   (divorced from instincts)

   (b) Concrete and abstract → Comprehensive mind, able to appreciate general principles

3. *Illumined Consciousness* → Comprehensive mind with flashes of illumination.

Hypnosis and pre-existence, or personality change?

In 1960 there was published a memorial volume to Knut Lundmark* which contained contributions by various authors. One by John Bjorkhem of Stockholm deals with twenty-five years study of the phenomenon of age regression under hypnotic influence. Regression in itself is nothing new, but these studies are significant in that they take the subject back to a time before he was born; in all cases a completely new personality emerges which has been termed the 'secondary personality'. Bjorkhem puts forward the theory that hypnosis provides a synthetic way of achieving one of the siddhis of Indian yogis (designated 'pubbe nivasanussatinana') whereby previous incarnations can be recalled to the waking consciousness. The significance of these experiments does not lie merely in psychological data but also in the philosophical and religious implications.

Some six hundred subjects have been studied embracing persons of all ages, occupations and intellectual standards. It was notable that every subject showed secondary personalities when the necessary hypnotic control was established—only in the case of very deep trance was normal intellectual activity so by-passed that no results could be obtained.

* *Knut Lundmark and Man's March into Space—a Memorial Volume*, published in Goteborg, 1961, as a memorial to Lundmark, Professor of Astronomy in the University of Lund, and which contains a number of articles by eminent men of science in English and Swedish.

The 'secondaries' manifest themselves with the same force and clarity whether the subject is ninety-five or only five years of age. An old person is taken back through different periods in his present life, then goes 'before birth' and is quite suddenly transformed into an entirely new person who tells about his life just as if he still existed. A seven-year-old who knows nothing of secondary personalities or theories of reincarnation is transformed and 'before birth' becomes an old man or woman telling quite naturally about his or her life in a way that implies experience of life foreign to a child of seven.

Other examples of such phenomena are given in *Les Vies Successives*, by Colonel Rochas d'Aiglun, Paris, 1911, and *The Search for Bridey Murphy*, by Morey Bernstein, U.S.A., 1956. That they occur cannot be denied, but their meaning and mechanism is still a matter for the sort of intensive study carried out by Bjorkhem.

An abnormal type of consciousness

During his work various points emerged which seem to have general validity. The subject's knowledge of the phenomenon of regression is without importance. Similarly, what the subject believes or does not believe has no effect on the results. The laws governing the phenomenon seem to operate independently on an entirely different plane from normal intellectual activity and act spontaneously when conditions are right. The less the change of consciousness under hypnosis the better will the subject remember the experience, but however intense it has been, recollection tends to fade rapidly unless it is fixed without delay in the memory; often, even intensive post-hypnotic suggestions fail to recall any perception unless a chance link is made.

The phenomenon always appears to the subject himself as a compulsive experience flowing from within, over which he has not the slightest control; one scene after another awakes with impartial questioning from the hypnotist; suggestions can take the scenes back freely through the centuries. Sometimes different languages appear and the subject talks fluently in a tongue normally unknown and even containing obsolete words and phrases. In some, the normal senses become acutely sensitive and even a whisper is painful. Sense perceptions in one half of the body can be totally extinguished or completely changed while the other half is altered in the opposite direction. A state of division sometimes exists whereby the normal consciousness observes what is developing from another stratum within, but is held in abeyance until the return to normal; it is the outer layer which is experienced as the normal self.

During regression, the voice changes, the face becomes rounder and movements become childish. Handwriting reverts to the appropriate period and if an epileptic subject is taken back to a period before the disease first manifested, it is not uncommon for the changes in the electroencephalogram which are typical of epileptics to disappear completely.

During regression to a very early age, perceptions sometimes appear without any intellectual interpretation, during the actual birth for example. The pure sensations are recalled and have to be interpreted by the now adult intelligence. Before the secondary appears there is nearly always a hiatus indicating temporary cessation of consciousness; dwelling on this period can produce intense feelings of anxiety in the subject.

Secondary personalities may be alternately men and women. A uniform technique with a harmonious subject almost always brings up the same personalities at the same periods of time, but actual dates are hard to determine; there are blank periods when no answers at all are given and the suggestions have to lead further back or forward in time to contact another personality. The intellectual standard of secondaries often bears no relation to that of the subject, dull subjects bringing up highly sarcastic, intelligent and witty personalities and highly intelligent subjects sometimes manifesting unintelligent secondaries, but normally the levels are more or less on a par.

Confusion of time, space and reality

One of the features of hypnotic consciousness is that it upsets the normal differentiation of time and space and reality. In trance there arise memories, conceptions and wishes with the same character as experienced reality itself. In regression there is thus no reliable criterion of what is really a reproduction of the individual's actual experiences and what was merely conceived in the mind. Both are held within the psyche and can be reproduced as real.

The whole hypnotic process is an opening up of the individual to suggestion; it puts in abeyance protections inherent in normal consciousness and permits direct injection of suggestions into the psychic apparatus so as to trigger off action under the psyche's own laws. Bjorkhem considers the chief function of normal consciousness to be the anchorage of the individual in a reality conditioned by space and time. Suggestion is thus the force that can lift the human consciousness out of these limitations. When a suggestion functions perfectly it is generally experienced as a force flowing through the whole organism with far-reaching effects. The ability to conceive a long-distant goal, formulate ideals and play the role that leads to them is the main feature distinguishing man from animal; the role acts as the guiding suggestion which makes the different elements in his being cohere, gives him dynamic force and makes him an entity with direction, and this role appears to be a pre-requisite for harmonious functioning of his psychic mechanisms.

Under hypnotic suggestion the role-assuming tendencies of the psyche seem to be aroused and past roles are reconstructed from stored material. No event from the past seems to be forgotten if it made an impression at the time; this is strikingly illustrated by the spontaneous reliving of past scenes when a person is on the point of drowning or in great danger. Mechanical stimulation of the brain is known to produce the same phenomenon and it seems that every phase of experience, every sense impression, is preserved intact and can be reproduced under the right conditions. But thoughts and feelings not based on actual experience have the same validity for the psyche as those that were, and thus roles are possible which bear little relation to facts of objective living.

A case is given of a lady regressing to 'before birth' who then gave an extremely detailed account of her own life and her husband's including a number of concrete and credible data. It finally proved that her information tallied with facts concerning the wife of her music teacher who had died some years previously. She very warmly appreciated her music teacher and it is not hard to understand how she came to choose that role. However, she had scarcely seen the person she represented and it was not possible to get any reliable idea of how the secondary personality collected the relevant data.

Despite the vast resources at the disposal of secondary personalities the same material is frequently produced with remarkable sureness and stringency, even after a lapse between experiments of twenty years.

Explanations of regression phenomena from the viewpoint of memory storage seem to become untenable when secondaries use obsolete language or display complete mastery of a foreign dialect in describing new happenings in the course of the experiment. Free use of grammatical speech in this way cannot be achieved by fragmentary phrases and expressions stored in a mechanical way.

Strange effects sometimes occur that are hardly amenable to investigation; for example a pain induced in one of the subject's arms may be described by him as occurring in the other. It may happen that a subject begins to write suddenly in double reversed mirror writing with a definiteness and firmness that eliminate the possibility of ordinary hysterical phenomena. Rather do such effects indicate that the human personality has latent possibilities at its disposal that are as good as unknown.

Bjorkhem suggests that further work should be done in two main categories:

(a) with subjects who produce the phenomenon when the waking consciousness is as little disturbed as possible and the secondary personality tends to be fragmentary;

(b) with those whose normal consciousness undergoes the profoundest change and who manifest incredibly well developed secondaries.

Persons who appear drawn to certain countries, historical epochs or cultures often produce secondaries with extremely characteristic attitudes and also the linguistic phenomena;

such people are of special interest despite the obvious possibility that their leanings may have prompted them to absorb detailed information into the conscious mind.

Subjects between eight and fifteen years of age are of interest because they are easy to handle and have limited mental conditioning and experience of life; a boy whose secondary shows the knowledge and understanding of an old man is all the more convincing. Young people who are stable and firm and open in nature cannot be harmed by properly conducted experiments of this sort, but any hostility to the idea can render them unco-operative and unsuitable for further investigation.

Finally Bjorkhem emphasises that regression phenomena may well represent the peak of attainment by hypnosis. It appears that once the waking consciousness is withheld from keeping biological man orientated firmly in time and space, his being responds to different laws which are little understood; essential contributions may be made to this understanding by further work along these lines.

Comments on this work by Bjorkhem

As a study of psychological mechanisms and the laws of the psyche, this hypnotic method may well produce valuable data. If it can establish the reality of a principle of life such as reincarnation, its benefit will be incalculable. Regression phenomena certainly occur, but there is no such certainty about their interpretation.

There seem to be three main alternatives to the theory that the secondaries are in fact the personalities of past lives. First the possibility Bjorkhem has already referred, to the acknowledged skill of the psyche in acting out a chosen role by selecting from its vast quantity of stored material.

How can the experimenter be sure that all the data brought forth relate solely to a certain past life of the subject and have not really been borrowed from other sources or even created anew? Accuracy in repetition is no problem for a perfect psychic memory.

Secondly the psyche is known to be able to separate itself into two or more independent parts, rather as in schizophrenia; in trance, hidden subdivisions sometimes come into action displaying completely different characteristics from that in evidence during normal conscious life. In other words this rival theory suggests that another self-contained part of the same individual is responsible for the whole phenomenon.

The third possibility is rather different. Natural safeguards are provided for the psyche by its being united firmly with the temporal consciousness, but if these are deliberately suspended by hypnosis and the psyche is told by suggestion to find another personality, it may take to itself any suitable psychic influence near at hand and display this as its own. The influence could be telepathically communicated from one or more living people, but if psychic characteristics are assumed to survive the physical body, there is no reason why the influence should not also be that of another psyche, now no longer incarnate.

The concept of reincarnation depends on such a belief that some part of a human being is permanent and survives physical dissolution. If this theory is on test by evidence from past lives, it will be necessary to prove that the secondary personalities are related directly to the past personalities of the subject and of no other entity. Deep trance subjects, in particular, may be open to psychic influences other than those relating to their own past lives.

Here there should be a warning: if such extraneous influences are possible, who can say that, once contacted, the psychic links are completely removed when the trance is ended and waking consciousness is apparently in control once more? With impeccable motives and great care, the dangers of venturing into this unknown territory will be minimised; but the risks attached to the research are not yet known and some heavy price may possibly be exacted from volunteers who expose themselves to experiments in a science which is still in its infancy, due to ignorance of the basic laws governing psychic activity. Hypnosis seems to be a most powerful tool with which to uncover important details about Man's nature and the potential rewards are great in terms of human understanding and advancement. Who shall say that the dangers are out of proportion? And even if they are, will there not always be those who dare anything in the quest for Truth?

Hypnosis as a tool in survivalist research

A comment on the previous article

In Bjorkhem's analysis of the hypnotic regression experiments performed under the aegis of Knut Lundmark, it is suggested in the third category of possible explanations for these supposedly reincarnationist phenomena that the psyche is capable of taking itself off, 'taking a suitable psychic influence near at hand, and displaying this as its own'. It is also suggested that if psychic characteristics do survive the physical body, then the influence utilised by the psyche could be from one now no longer incarnate.

This is a desperately important point in this field of psychic research, and there have recently been published some most relevant findings from other hypnotic regression experiments. The more thorough investigations into the background of the Bridey Murphy case showed that Bernstein's wife had associated with Irish immigrants during her early childhood, and that all the actual verifiable issues were categorically incorrect, and far more likely to have been uninspired guesses. The alternative explanations are well described by Martin Gardner.

Edwin Zolik, who has been working on a programme of experiments since 1955, has come to the conclusion that when the crucial elements of the 'previous existence' (or 'progignomatic' as he has named it) phenomenon are fully investigated, they reveal a dynamic relationship between the subject's personality and his 'previous existence' fantasy.

Further, the fantasy appears to serve as a screen on to which would be projected the important motivational systems of the personality.

Subjects used in the series were first screened for psychiatric or psychological disorder, and only accepted if they could achieve within four training sessions a satisfactory degree of trance. For each subject two sessions were held; in the first the subject, in a deep hypnotic state, was regressed and, when possible, a progignomatic fantasy elicited. A post-hypnotic suggestion of complete amnesia for this session followed. If a suitable fantasy were elicited, and complete amnesia achieved, then a second session was held one week later, when the possible sources of the fantasy were explored without inducing age-regression. This exploration was non-directive, and free-association was encouraged.

One subject provided a typical, and very excellent, object-lesson as to the origin of these fantasies. He described himself with considerable and convincing detail as 'Brian O'Malley', a British soldier serving in the Irish Guards about 1850. He described his death in an accident with a horse, and details of the time reminiscent of the quality of Bridey Murphy's. At the second session he was asked whether he knew anything of this man, and he then described how a man of that name had fought with his grandfather while the subject was a young child, and how O'Malley had later been killed while riding a horse. It appeared that his grandfather particularly hated this man, and the fantasy was dynamically related in the subject's mind to a major emotional conflict, quasi-Oedipal in nature, and not completely resolved. Before the session ended the subject was given the post-hypnotic suggestion that he would be able to recall only the material he wished to recall, and upon awakening recall was complete. Since the fantasy resulted in the return of repressed unconscious material, supportive therapy was given until recovery was complete.

Zolik goes on to argue forcibly that the fantasy was being enacted as an unconscious hostility reaction against the subject's grandfather, whom he had certain reasons to both hate and fear. Further, in his job he was creating needless conflict by expressing hostility towards his immediate superiors; in other subjects, the fantasies depicted conflicts of which the subjects were at least partially aware. The fantasies were consistently related to factors in the subject's experiential background, but in no instance could they be discussed as manifestations of multiple personality. This study does, therefore, underline the need for the most thorough analysis of the material brought out during regression experiments.

Dissociated memory

The question of cryptamnesia* is now receiving more attention in para-psychological journals, and the concept of alleged 'former memories' that are displaced and disguised memories of former childhood that this term implies, may yet yield useful information. Dr. C. Chari has pointed out that when very small children, who have not even talked or learnt to read properly, offer evidence of a survivalist character, the cryptamnesic hypothesis may appear to lose some of its pertinence. In India it has been noted that Indian children, who accompany their mother on her visits

---

* Cryptamnesia: memory without identification or recognition as previous experience, the original experience having been forgotten or repressed, leading to reinstatement of the memory as apparently new experience.

to neighbours and temples from an early age, have a more developed perception of adult attitudes than American children of the same age. This may help to explain why a number of Indian children have recently been the object of 'survivalist' investigations; this, however, has been vehemently denied by Dr. Ian Stevenson of the University of Virginia.

A more basic problem than this is, however, revealed, for do memories of very early infancy exist at all? Dr. Francis Scott successfully drew the pattern of a wallpaper he saw when only three months old, but descriptions of regression earlier than this may always be confused with the imaginative powers of the subconscious.

In the 1957–1958 *Journal of Psychology*, Dr. Theodore Barber argues the case for believing that when a subject is age-regressed to six months old, his behaviour will be in accordance with his perception of himself as a six-month-old infant. A good hypnotic subject can be induced to commit anti-social or dangerous acts if his perceptions and conceptions are altered in such a way that he believes the behaviour to be normal and proper in the suggested circumstances. By dint of definition and experience it is known that a subject is not in a deep state of hypnotic trance unless he believes that the operator's words are true statements.

A good subject quickly becomes a poor one when he realises that the hypnotist does not have any special power or ability to make him believe anything he does not wish to believe. The psychology of hypnosis is therefore related inextricably to the psychology of belief and perception. Barber goes on to suggest that good hypnotic subjects have certain features in common that set them apart from the average; they are persons who have the habit of becoming

P

relatively detached and unconcerned about their surroundings; they are all apt to fall into abstractions or reveries,
or are able to concentrate on their work by 'blocking out'
environmental stimuli. With rare exceptions, they are
persons easily able to go to sleep at any time or place. They
also tend to strive to behave like a hypnotised person as this
is continuously defined by the operator and understood by
the subject. Thus, even in the conscious state, a good subject
has a natural tendency towards role-assumption. It must be
remembered that really good subjects represent only a
fraction of the community, and the many confusing factors
make it necessary to examine any testimony of 'Former
Lives' with scrupulous care.

References

The International Journal of Parapsychology, Vol. IV, Nos. 3
    and 4.
The Science Group Journal, December 1962.
Fads and Fallacies of Science, Martin Gardner, Doubleday,
    New York.

Hypnosis and the unconscious

It has been mentioned earlier that the mind, in the parts of the unconscious which are not far from the line dividing conscious and unconscious is so organised—presumably having become so in the course of long evolutionary development—that it is as though a creature were living with us. That creature, whom we have previously called 'George', is between us and the rest of the universe 'within'; he is between us and 'mind at large', to use again Aldous Huxley's phrase; 'Mind at large' includes all the 'higher planes' of classical theosophical literature.

'George' has many activities: he sorts, classifies, collates, pigeon-holes. He is in charge of the memory store. He sometimes passes up to us in the conscious mind (functioning here through the physical brain) information acquired at his level (the psychic level) or from deeper levels. He has psychic faculties; a 'psychic' is a person whose 'George' is able readily to pass up information through a permanent or semi-permanent channel. Some people are born with these channels open—born psychic—while others develop them by training and by altering the body chemistry through religious or meditative practices or by taking drugs.

'George' is used to handling the data of the physical world, the information of the senses, and he usually can give information to us only in this form. If he acquires a deep spiritual truth, or a message of encouragement from a 'higher sense' (deep in what is, for most of us at our stage of evolutionary development, the unconscious) he is obliged to symbolise it, that is, express it in terms of the objects of the physical world, in order to pass it on. This is the only language he knows.

Hypnosis is a state of increased suggestibility in which the critical faculty of the conscious mind is partially or wholly in abeyance. Suggestions can, under certain conditions, be accepted and go straight to 'George'. The hypnotic state is a state of direct contact with 'George'. It can be brought about in a number of different ways and can then produce very remarkable results.

This state of hypnosis can be induced by someone else—if the subject co-operates—or it can be brought about by one-self, in which case it is called auto-hypnosis. Auto-hypnosis can result from intense concentration; or by the repeated recitation of a mantram; or by the use of a koan until the conscious mind becomes dizzy and stops working.

In this state of quiescence of the conscious mind, 'George' will dramatise various experiences, in fact 'George' is most obliging. If we believe in reincarnation and investigate this doctrine, perhaps by a time-regression technique, in which the hypnotised subject is told that he is going backwards in time, becoming in stages a young person, a small child and so on into the womb and ultimately back into former lives —'George' will co-operate. He will produce pseudo-details of past lives. 'George' will acquire whatever useful information he can—from our memory store of things read or over-heard, consciously remembered, or forgotten, or by using his extra-sensory perception—and he will dramatise it in order to help us 'prove' reincarnation. *The Search for Bridey Murphy*, by Morey Bernstein, is probably an example of 'George's' activities, and so possibly is *The Lives of Alcyone*, by Annie Besant and C. W. Leadbeater. 'George' will do this quite independently of whether reincarnation is true or not.

The 'training' of a medium is a training of 'George'. He behaves according to his training. Believing whatever we tell him firmly enough, he will symbolise or dramatise accordingly. Clairvoyance and clairaudience are examples of 'George's' dramatisation, in which he puts information obtained by E.S.P. into terms of the physical body senses of seeing and hearing. He may have obtained that information from the memory store of the medium's sitter, or from someone in the next world, or otherwise: it is often not possible to tell.

In sleep and in day-dreaming and in sensory deprivation experiments, 'George' is often given a free rein. He has no constant stream of sensory information to deal with and so is able to play games with what material he has to hand. He sometimes produces fantastic dreams woven out of memories. These dreams can tell a psychiatrist a lot about 'George's' little habits and prejudices. Sometimes these dreams are mixed up with valuable information from the deeper levels of consciousness where time is quite different: this information is occasionally of matters lying in the future to the ordinary brain consciousness. 'George' has to symbolise all this information; sometimes he gets it muddled.

If 'George' has all these interesting powers, perhaps he can be trained to use them. The March 1962 *Journal of The Society for Psychical Research* contains a paper dealing with just that, and describes a piece of work, mentioned briefly earlier in *Psychism and the Mind*, which may represent an important break-through in psychical research. The paper is entitled, 'Training the Psi Faculty by Hypnosis'. In this paper is described how Dr. Milan Ryzl took a number of perfectly ordinary people and achieved, through training under hypnosis, a 'relatively good clairvoyant ability' in about 27 persons out of a total of 226. A lesser clairvoyant ability was obtained in 29 persons; the failures totalled 170, that is 75%. The success of the E.S.P. was measured statistically and in other ways.

Dr. Ryzl's last subject was a twenty-two-year-old girl who worked in an office and had never experienced E.S.P. His method was as follows. He first hypnotised her and suggested various delusions of the senses. He later suggested visions of various kinds, often of places where she had been. The visions were made sharp and clear and changeable at will by appropriate suggestions. Having reached this point, Dr. Ryzl would ask for a piece of information the subject had not consciously registered when originally at the place of the vision. Means for distinguishing between true and false hallucinations were found, the brightness of the vision to the subject being the most important factor.

Dr. Ryzl next taught her to observe objects with her eyes shut, *immediately* checking to correct false impressions. The objects were moved behind screens and then to greater distances. Ultimately, for objects in other rooms, she developed 'travelling clairvoyance', that is, she had out-of-the-body experiences.

The hypnotic trance was gradually brought under the subject's own volition, so that she could hypnotise herself, with the necessary inhibition of thought for E.S.P., and deepen and terminate it at will. In other words, she could hypnotise herself, *use* the developed E.S.P. facility, and then remember the result after return to normal consciousness.

Her ability gradually became wider in scope. After a month, the ability to read other people's thoughts appeared spontaneously. Telepathy came most easily from the marginal zones of consciousness. She was able to find missing objects. It will be noted that this girl appeared to obtain most of the *siddhis*—the psychic faculties which arise during yoga training.

However, it is not clear how many of her visions were obtained by telepathy, or in some instances by unconscious dramatisation; certainly no precautions were taken to exlude the operation of precognitive telepathy.

This research, conducted with great skill by Dr. Ryzl and involving a large number of subjects, has shown that by means of hypnosis it is possible to train the E.S.P. ability in some people to such an extent that it is governable by will and applicable as an additional sense.

There are some final points on this subject of 'George' which need to be considered by those who practise meditation. While holding one's mind still in the quietude of one's room, and trying to 'raise one's consciousness', it is possible occasionally to slip into a state of auto-hypnosis. If this condition is entered with fixed ideas as to what is likely to happen, it is probable that the experience gained will correspond exactly with one's preconceived ideas.

It is stated in books on occultism that those who die with fixed ideas as to what they are likely to find in the next world, usually get the experiences they expect. Similarly if in an auto-hypnotic state they appear to enter an interesting part of the astral plane, it does not necessarily indicate that an expansion of consciousness has taken place. Nor if one seems to leave one's body and travel about in that attractive world, does it follow that this is more than the active dramatising effect of 'George'. However, owing to the elevated state of mind of the aspirant, the experience may lead to valuable teaching being given apparently from someone in that world, but that teaching will in fact have come from a much higher level, since the astral world is no more spiritual than the physical.

Having reached this stage it is important not to be deflected by the attractive experiences of the astral world, but to persevere with regular periods of meditation, until at some point one may have a flash of Buddhic consciousness with its ineffable bliss and sense of unity with all creation. At such a moment one knows with certainty that all life is one, and that a real expansion of consciousness has taken place. This is the first aim of Raja Yoga.

Such an experience cannot be brought about by hypnotic suggestion, but needs the positive stilling of the mind, and shutting off of the five senses, while turning one's attention inwards. This is the first step of a long stairway to the highest, but one must guard against stepping off too soon, or proceeding with fixed ideas as to what will be found at different levels of the stairway.

Each step must be taken as a child, wide-eyed, innocent and with an open mind: and who knows what treasure will be found? Those who express it do not know. Those who know cannot express it.

The issue of the consciousness-expanding drugs

Based on an article by W. W. Harman in *Main Currents in Modern Thought*, September 1963

While some authorities are hailing the new psychedelic* or consciousness expanding drugs as a wonderful new therapeutic tool for the treatment of phobic states, certain neuroses, and neurotic psychopaths, others are pointing out that they are too powerful and too controversial to be used for research in a university setting, and they have not been the subject of any major university study in America. Controversy rages over whether they are truly 'consciousness-expanding' or merely 'mind-distorting' in their fundamental action, and whether it is right to assume that insights obtained under psychologically abnormal conditions can have true and valid meaning. It has been suggested that lysergic acid (LSD)—one of the principle drugs of this group—can induce striking alterations in behaviour, and in many patients induce a 'mystical experience' in which they may obtain startling insights into their problems.

Many experts feel that it is hard to distinguish between what could be termed a drug-induced freeing of the mind, and a corresponding therapist-induced mystical experience similar to religious conversion. There is no doubt that suggestibility plays a major role in determining the nature of the experience provided by these drugs, and it should be

* Psychedelic means literally—mind manifesting.

remembered that during the widespread use of related materials in religious exercises throughout the world for centuries, the setting was always deliberately contrived to remind the partaker that the hallowed ground of his own soul was being made accessible to him.

This does not necessarily invalidate the patient's experience, any more than an aesthetic experience is invalidated because others considered a particular work of art to be beautiful, or the psychiatric patient's insight because he had once read Freud. It is well known that such patients are able to 'pick up' the conceptual framework of a person who is with them during a session, and therefore one must distinguish between authentic experience and appropriate dogma when present.

It is true to say that these drugs do have the ability to expand the range of conscious awareness, but it affects matters real as much as those that are imaginary. The experience may be conveniently divided into three states:

1. An *evasive stage*, in which the strange new feelings and perceptions that are flooding in induce a state of great confusion, and any distrust of others becomes magnified into a paranoidal sort of suspicion and anxiety; hallucinations may occur, in vivid colour sometimes, or take the form of abstract symbols that may become fraught with meaning as the individual moves into

2. the *symbolic stage*: the insights obtained are of a more generalised philosophico-religious nature, and may come as a newly deepened significance to a familiar phrase such as 'We are all one', or in an awareness of a greatly intensified feeling or relationship to others and to the entire universe. By relinquishing his concepts and surrendering himself to the

experience he finds he can move beyond the state where knowledge is mediated in symbolic form, to a totally new condition in which it appears directly.

3. Stage of *immediate perception*: the individual develops an awareness of other aspects of reality than those to which he is accustomed, and he may attempt to describe 'levels of consciousness' or 'other dimensions of space', but even while speaking recognises the effort of description to be as doomed to partial failure as the effort to describe being in love to someone who has not experienced it. He may find the age-old question 'Who am I?' does have a significant answer, and because the new knowledge of himself has been gained as a deeply felt experience and not merely by an intellectual exercise, his later behaviour does tend to become more appropriate to his expanded picture of himself.

Thus persons who do not move beyond the first stage will have a very different experience from those who reach the second one, and find therein a source of fantasy and emotional material more controllable than dreams; those who reach the third stage talk of 'liberation therapy' in terms analagous to the 'unitive knowing' or 'new kind of consciousness' characteristic of mystical experience. Often, when the experts themselves take these drugs they do not share these latter experiences, nor the enthusiasms of their patients.

It may be contended that suggestibility plays such a major role in the outcome of the experience, that it should be deplored as an 'artificial' aid to spirituality or enlightenment, yet we would not apply this adjective to liturgy, religious symbol, meditation techniques, fasting or asceticism. The basic issue is perhaps more evasive and subtle. It is really the threat posed by the fact that if one considers psychedelic experience to be essentially valid, this implies that the belief and value system implicit in our 'scientific' culture is not uniquely true and not even optimally wholesome.

Psychological defence mechanisms

Let us consider now a definition of what is meant by 'belief-and-value system': it is no more than the total network of psycho-analytical defence mechanisms organised together to form a cognitive system and designed to shield a vulnerable mind. It is in terms of such a definition that we can find most comprehensible the historical instances where new theories to accommodate existing data have resulted in controversies in which both sides have shown unusual personal involvement and emotional vigour. Over the years we have perhaps learnt to be comfortable with the phenomena in spite of the lack of an adequate theory.

With respect to these drugs, the data that are most recalcitrant towards containment in the old conceptual framework are the seeming universality of the psychedelic perception, which points to its relationship with mystical experience. However, it is not claimed that all LSD-experience is mystical, but only that some *may* be. It gives one a splendid flash of what can be, and what one must surely aim for. It resolves the goal, and the goal is found worthy of pursuit. Thoughts arising from the third stage seem to hit with absolute truth from nowhere—not the result of analysing. The more accounts one examines, the harder it is to escape from the conclusion that there is a basic human experience, with qualities or attributes which are universal in the sense that they are independent of culture and conditioning, and of the suggestibility factor in the environment. One important therapeutic result that so often comes up, is a new attitude to death; it would be difficult to estimate how much the fear of non-existence enters into psychotherapy—suffice it to say that it is a key problem. What death negates is not the individual, not the organism/environment, but the ego, and therefore liberation of the ego is synonymous with full acceptance of death. The LSD patient will laugh at the false problem (if he has achieved the third stage), since he sees that he couldn't non-exist if he wanted to.

Subjects who have been asked to re-assess their belief-systems at the end of therapy, very often show deep-seated convictions when presented with mystically-worded statements—e.g. 'Man is in essence eternal and infinite'. They are therefore in effect saying that they are convinced of the possibility of gaining valid knowledge through an extra-sensory mode of perception. Thus the person who feels a compulsion to explain away all E.S.P. data will also find the LSD subject to be the victim of delusion and hallucination.

Truth is ineluctable

If we accept St. Exupery's statement that 'truth is not that which is demonstrable—it is that which is ineluctable', then we can perhaps regard man's unconscious processes as revealed by these drugs to be both 'a goldmine as well as a rubbish heap' as Myers suggested. Traditionally the experience of gnosis, of direct perception and knowledge, has been among the most highly prized of human experiences, and traditionally the knowledge is not easily won. However, we may arrive at a new concept of gnosis if we can look upon psychedelic drugs as but one way to follow the dictum—'Know thyself'.

In the same issue of *Main Currents in Modern Thought* there are certain pertinent comments in an article entitled 'A Modern Approach to Mystical Experience' by U. Asrani. He makes the point that drugs have been used in all ages and all cultures as an aid to mystical experience; reference is made to them in the Rig Veda, and many mystics rightly or wrongly tolerated the use of drugs—Patanjali himself mentioned that they *may* be an alternative method for the achievement of the initial stages. He included many physiological practices in his modes of preparation, but stressed that they were not the goal itself. Asrani criticises the idea that drugs could lead to real insight or spirituality because the subject is always merely passive or receptive; the expanded wellbeing felt by the subject is not his own achievement, self-engendered and self-controlled. Further, the continued use of drugs is always subject to the law of diminishing returns, and LSD does not appear to be an exception, whereas the more traditional routes to spirituality are more truly progressive.

Disintegrating effect of psychedelic drugs

The large majority of people feel that the struggle to attain personal insight is not merely a self-centred or selfish pursuit, but something that can result in benefit to all humanity. In contrast, these drugs have been shown to have a disintegrating effect on both inborn and learned patterns in both animals and man. When given to garden spiders, they produced severe faults in web-building, fish become disorientated, and mammals appear to lose interest in their surroundings and to respond feebly to hostile stimuli. In man LSD produces blocking and indifferent performance in tests that evaluate memory, attention and manual dexterity; perhaps most important of all, motivation is impaired, and this is one quality that must be kept vitally active if the drug is to be used for any spiritual end (1).

In clinical assessment it has been found that the effect is enhanced by sensory deprivation, and this is consistent with the comparison between patients under LSD and those who suffer from temporal lobe epilepsy, a condition in which there is a heightened memory for past events, and a sense of being able to understand everything. The existence of this component of psychopathology has led to suggestions that the drug should only be given to patients when they can be offered special care and social welfare observation, such as could be offered by special clinics working apart from the main hospitals.

Gordon Wasson in a recent article (2) suggests that Mescaline puts many within reach of the state achieved by the mystics without having to suffer the mortifications of Blake or St. John; this, however, is an aesthetic addition to our lives, and should not be regarded as one of spiritual achievement, even though the be-mushroomed Mexican eating his Peyotl may appear to be undergoing a 'soul-shattering' experience.

In the ancient disciplines of Yoga and Zen Buddhism the opposite courses of attachment and detachment from sensory stimuli are used, with the aim of surmounting the barriers of selfhood and, by by-passing the usual processes of logical thinking, extend the individual's awareness of his own deeper levels of consciousness. To such disciplines the psychedelic drugs could be a useful adjunct.

In the sphere of E.S.P. research the drug LSD is being spoken of with great enthusiasm. Duncan Blewett (*American*

Journal of Parapsychology, Vol. V, No. 1) describes experimental work that has been done using subjects who have been offered special guidance during their first few sessions, by someone who has already established order and organisation in the unhabitual aspects of experience induced by it. They appear to overcome the initial confusional states very quickly, and learn to analyse the mass of incoming sensations at great speed, and exert some control over the inrush which causes the peculiar disturbances of time-sense (cf. Christopher Mayhew's experience of the drug). Once the subjects are fully stabilised to the experience and to the confusing effect of testing procedures, it becomes possible to give the drug to a group of subjects, and elicit a remarkable increase in the proximity of feeling between the participants. This sensitisation to the effect of empathy promises to permit extensive investigation of the transfer (including non-verbal transfer) of feeling that is produced in this state, in which the ability to communicate appears to verge on the telepathic.

References

1. The deeper social implications are dealt with in *The Significance of the Mind Changing Drugs* by Emily Sellon, The Theosophical Press, Wheaton, Illinois.
2. *International Journal of Parapsychology*, Autumn, 1962.

Can drugs bring wisdom?

It seems appropriate to offer some further comments, from religious and theosophical viewpoints, on the use of psychedelic drugs. The controversy as to whether they should be encouraged or banned has aroused exceptionally strong feelings on both sides, and this is not surprising in the light of the fundamental personality changes these drugs can sometimes induce.

Curiously, opposition arises from at least three quite different standpoints. In the main it comes from those inclined towards a philosophy based on relatively materialistic science; such people have a vested interest in the established order of things, at psychological as well as material levels. Drug-induced experiences akin to the mystical, which throw grave doubts upon its ultimate truth and value, are thoroughly unwelcome. If they are false and delusional then they are dangerous to the individual and society and should be suppressed. But the unshakable conviction with which some of the subjects hold their newly-revealed beliefs makes such facile dismissal unconvincing; yet it would be altogether too upsetting to admit the possible validity of these beliefs, so again the means to acquire them should be quietly banned. Such opposition comes from those who would welcome the crucifixion of Jesus, should he come again.

However, criticism of this attitude must not be construed as approval for indiscriminate use of psychedelic drugs. There are without doubt many people, the majority probably, who would get nothing from them but a mainly

Q

unpleasant experience. Some would be terrified and suffer more or less permanent psychological damage. Medical opposition on the grounds of danger to health and sanity is sincere and should not lightly be set aside.

There exists also a third group of people, who are genuinely puzzled and distressed by the more profound effects of these drugs. These are sincerely religious persons, or those who have embraced Eastern philosophies, and who thoroughly accept the validity of the mystical experience and earnestly desire to achieve it themselves. To this end they may undertake, over many years, ascetic practices and regular meditation or some form of Yoga. To them it seems unreasonable, unjust and undesirable that their cherished objective can sometimes be attained just by swallowing a drug. Experience thus gained by cheating, as it were, must surely be false in some way, or if true, then it seems to make a mockery of their teachings and practices.

Those who desire unrestricted access to the drugs similarly comprise at least three distinct groups. The deplorable majority want them just 'for kicks', though many of them will not enjoy the kicks they receive. The second group wish to use the drugs in a responsible manner, in a spirit of scientific enquiry. The third see themselves as devotees of an up-to-date scientifically-based mushroom cult; they also employ them with due responsibility and in appropriate circumstances, seeking truth through expansion of consciousness. Some of these people too, though they may achieve their ultimate objective, may not really welcome the soul-shattering mystical experience when it comes. For it is profoundly disturbing to be uplifted so far and so literally out of oneself. In this unfamiliar condition, truth does not appear as an intellectual idea one is free to take or leave. Indeed, it can neither be taken nor left, but itself sweeps one up into its embrace. For the instant one has no identity outside this revelation. Moreover, one is thenceforth condemned to live with the vivid memory of that ecstacy, and in its light the old selfish ways of life seem sinful, as they did not before.

There must be some explanation of the fact that a sip of LSD may induce a deeper experience of instant Grace than the communion cup. Earnest people work hard at living the spiritual life as if it were a new skill to be learned. So it is in one sense, but the greater part of it is really a matter of *un*learning. It is first necessary, though difficult, to discard many of the socially-approved opinions and habits acquired during a lifetime in the 'rat-race', for such mental conditioning chains one down and prevents one's soul rising to the heights.

Once this is appreciated it becomes easier to see how a drug might help. For whereas it is hard to imagine how it could create positive conditions assumed to be necessary for the break-through, a negative effect of suppressing hindrances and by-passing inhibitions is understandable. This is merely an extension of what can be accomplished by other substances like alcohol, sedatives and tranquilisers. Even without assistance from drugs, moreover, deliberate preparation by meditation and yoga is certainly not always necessary, for the experience has come to many people spontaneously and unbidden, or following an emotional shock. Examples have been collected by Bucke in his book *Cosmic Consciousness*. Nevertheless it seems likely that such individuals had really been making preparations unconsciously through a religious or philosophical attitude or a naturally benevolent disposition. It seems that conscious-ness-expanding drugs likewise cannot manifest their full potential without such conscious or unconscious preparation. So there is no cheating or miracle involved in their use; they merely effect temporary release from the few remaining inhibitions, leaving the consciousness open and receptive to inspiration.

As described in 'The difference between spiritual and psychic perception' in Section III, the intuitive perceptions may stop short of the complete union of yoga, or cosmic consciousness.

Materialists are puzzled by the intense conviction of subjects that ultimate truth has been revealed to them. But all the great religions testify to a supreme reality far beyond comprehension by our normal earthbound intelligence. Mystics may claim to have seen God, or to have received absolute total truth, but, however wondrous the experience, they have entered into only such fragment of that reality as they can appreciate, we can be sure that full understanding is still way ahead.

Finally, the pragmatist may ask whether such experiences are desirable in today's world. The answer has to be yes, for tomorrow's world must be very different and will allow full scope for altruism. Western civilisation encourages competitiveness, ambition and aggressiveness. One must seek one's own advantage and 'get on in the world', inevitably to the disadvantage of the less successful. So one tends to develop a hard skin of indifference. One's finer feelings are set aside to avert painful conflict, and they tend to atrophy. With such intense concentration on material prosperity, religious observances have fallen into disuse, and the religious spirit itself seems to be in decline.

All this may be a necessary stage in the course of human evolution, but it surely is not the last. The far-sighted have already seen that humanity, individually and collectively, is approaching a fundamental turning point in evolution. Our very successes in agriculture and industry and military might must compel a gradual reversal of attitude from competition to co-operation and mutual aid. This is starting already, but it is still hard to imagine what this new world will be like. The several Utopias so far envisaged have not seemed convincing. A recent one where psychedelic drugs are used, with due discretion, is depicted in Aldous Huxley's novel *Island*. In any event, to guide these stupendous changes, and to bring them about before disaster overtakes us, will surely call for leaders with spiritual insight.

The role of the mind in the success of unrelated methods of healing

It is interesting to consider some of the numerous anomalies which occur in the process of treating the sick, and to see if there is any common factor that can be found in the different methods, both orthodox and unorthodox, used with success in treating the same ailment.

Most people are aware of the rivalry between homeopathy and orthodox medicine, how in the latter system potent chemicals are used which alter the metabolism of the body, modify the activity of various organs, or attack bacteria and other invading parasites which appear to be the cause of certain illnesses: while in homeopathy infinitely small amounts of active substances are used, and often diluted to such a high degree that it can be proved the final tablet or liquid which the patient is given does not contain one single molecule of the original substance! In spite of this, both methods of treatment which are so completely different in conception and technique get their successes.

Then there is the school of osteopathy which considers all illnesses to be due to minute displacements of the spinal vertebrae which cause pressure on the nerves emerging from the spinal cord, and thus cause interference with the vitality of the respective organs of the body with which they are connected. In such cases, treatment consists of adjusting the appropriate region of the vertebral column by manipulation.

Successes with fundamentally different treatments

There are numerous other methods of treatment, all of which have their ardent advocates, and which can claim many successes. One of the most popular at the present time is radiesthesia, in which the patient supplies a drop of dried blood or saliva on a piece of filter paper, which the practitioner places in a piece of apparatus which he claims enables him to determine the specific vibration or vibrations of the disease in question, and so enables him to diagnose what is wrong with the patient, who need not be present. Having made a diagnosis, the radiesthesist passes an electric current through his apparatus in a way that he claims will radiate through space to the patient the compensatory vibrations needed to counteract the disease vibrations.

The practitioners of this system go further and claim that they can diagnose disease in its very earliest stages, before it has caused any symptoms of any kind, and by sending out the correct radiation to the patient, can neutralise the disease before it has manifested itself. In this way, it is said that a person who is perfectly healthy and active can be cured of a disease they do not have at the time, but would have in the future if they did not take a suitable course of radiesthesia!

There are numerous other healing systems based on different theories, such as the ancient Chinese method of acupuncture which has suddenly become fashionable, or the wearing of different kinds of charms, or even the burying in the garden of a piece of bacon-rind at the exact moment of the Full Moon!

Now the interesting point about all these methods of diagnosis and treatment is that in spite of the fact that the theories on which they are based may be quite antagonistic, or apparently absurd, *they all have their successes*. Moreover, there are numerous cases on record where treatment has failed when carried out by clever physicians with considerable knowledge, which have later been cured by less orthodox methods, some of which seem to be based on pure superstition.

These undisputed facts force one to look deeper for the causes of human ailments, but before we can discover the factor or factors common to these very diverse methods of treatment, we must consider the constitution of man in his totality.

This takes us far back into the evolution of the animal kingdom, which provided us with the physical bodies we inhabit today.

The evolutionary perfection of the physical body

The mammalian body is probably the most wonderful creation of evolution on this planet, and it has taken very many millions of years to reach this degree of perfection.

It is remarkably complex, yet works with such superb harmony that in its natural animal state it enjoys perfect, unselfconscious, health. All its functions are controlled by an elaborate system of reflexes, working on a plan of the utmost wisdom, which enables the animal to satisfy all its needs in the ever-changing environment in which it finds itself. If it is injured by accident or attack, its tissues and bones have latent powers of self-regeneration which come into play the moment an injury occurs. If harmful bacteria or viruses invade its body, its highly complex and well organised chemical system creates the exact specific antibody which will kill the invader but do no damage to its own living cells; moreover, once it has had such an experience, it stores up an excess of the antibodies it has manufactured, in order to be still more prepared for a future attack by the same micro-organisms, should it occur.

If seasonal changes in its environment necessitate its moving to other parts of the globe, the highly sensitive reflexes in its controlling nervous centre cause it to migrate to those parts most suited to its needs.

And lastly, in order that its particular species shall not become extinct, elaborate systems of hormone stimuli enable it to reproduce its kind at times and in circumstances which give greatest protection to its young.

All these things take place instinctively, and unselfconsciously, always adjusting themselves to fortuitous changes that may take place at any time, so that any contingency that may arise—apart from something catastrophic—is provided for in a remarkably comprehensive way that only a tremendous intelligence could have devised.

At the same time as the physical body evolves, the animal develops an emotional system which helps it to create the subtler reflexes needed for the finer adjustments of its daily life.

Such feelings as pain, fear and alertness, help to protect it from external dangers, while affection and protectiveness cause it to preserve the family unit. Nourishment and rest are controlled by hunger and fatigue, and the joy of living acts as a general incentive to healthy activity.

When this physical animal body with its attendant emotional mechanism finally reached perfection, Man took charge of it for himself, and added to it his selfconscious mind—a mind having the power to overrule the natural instincts of the body. But whereas his body was the result of millions of years of experience, his mind was a new and untried instrument, lacking both wisdom and experience, and thus causing a state of unbalance from the very beginning of his existence.

Conflict between body and mind

This struggle between mind and body still obtains today, and it seems that Man's main purpose at this stage of his cosmic evolution is to bring his conscious mind to the same state of perfection as that of his unconscious body, so that the two will work in harmony, and not as antagonists, as so frequently happens.

When there is strain between body and mind, the forces of life welling up deeply within are obstructed in varying degrees and at different levels as they flow outwards. Such impediments to the passage of vitality cause weakness and congestion at the sites of obstruction, giving rise to ill-health at those particular levels, and can be brought about in many different ways.

Primitive Man, with his perfect physical instrument, but untried mind, is impatient and anxious to exercise the latter's powers and experiment with life. Unfortunately he lacks wisdom and experience, and so does many foolish things, interfering with the harmony of himself and the surroundings in which he lives, indulging his sensations for the pleasure and excitement they bring, rather than using them as a guide to the needs of his body. This leads to pain and ill-health at the levels of his being where he has gone astray, and so the forces of reaction are called into play and gradually compel him to seek out his errors and remedy the disharmony he has created, thus bringing him back once more to a state of good health.

Now the very nature of the inertia and density of physical

matter necessitates a great effort on the part of the spirit of
man to bring about such an adjustment, and the magnitude
of this effort impresses his inner nature with the importance
of all the factors concerned, so that they become a permanent
part of him—in fact, a small fragment of wisdom—and in
this way he evolves.

Illness is beneficent

Illness from a broader viewpoint is thus seen to be a beneficent adjusting process of the inner man bringing about
spiritual harmony, and not just a matter of bad luck or
misfortune.

Health, like everything else in life, follows basic laws of
cause and effect, so it is impossible to go against these laws
and then think that some new healing method, or wonder
drug, will quickly restore good health and excuse one from
dealing with the original mistakes. Nature cannot be de-
ceived or bribed, but she welcomes co-operation in her
work.

It follows from this that all disease is psychosomatic when
viewed fundamentally, though this is by no means always
apparent, owing to the difficulty, at times, of discerning at
what level of man's complex being the flow of life has been
obstructed and led to the manifestation of a particular illness.

Yet the list of physical ailments recognised by orthodox
medicine as being psychosomatic grows longer almost daily
as the relationship between man's psyche and his ailments
continues to become clearer.

To mention just a few of the commoner complaints,
gastric and duodenal ulcers, caused by prolonged anxiety,
perhaps head the list. Asthma and eczema are often due to
deep unconscious fear of some aspect of life, while a raised

blood pressure with its secondary ill effects of haemorrhage and paralysis can be brought about by prolonged worry at the conscious level; and even simple obesity often results from seeking, by over-eating, a happiness in life that is otherwise lacking.

In all these cases so far we have been considering chronic diseases, but when we look at acute infections, they seem to be distinctly physical, without any traces of mental origins. However, on deeper consideration we find that the continuous ignoring of simple laws of health such as overworking, over-indulgence, lack of fresh air or exercise, will ultimately bring about an acute illness owing to the accumulation of toxic products in the system; then, pathogenic micro-organisms of various kinds may take an active part by living on these accumulated waste products, and in turn add their own toxic substances to the total mass of poisons. Treatment in such cases is often begun by administering eliminating remedies and antibiotics or similar substances to destroy the infecting bacteria, or to hold up their rapid multiplication until the body has had time to develop its defences. In this way a severe case of pneumonia may be prevented from reaching a fatal termination by the administration of penicillin in the early stages, but the fact that the penicillin has not cured the disease can be seen by the long convalescence which follows—it has simply gained time by stopping a rapid chain reaction.

Chronic psychosomatic diseases

Returning to chronic psychosomatic cases, the co-operation of the patient is vital if a cure is to be effected. With a certain amount of self-examination, and sympathetic assistance from the healer, he may often discover some habit; or rigid attitude of mind; or discord in his life; which is acting as a vital obstruction and is the main cause of his trouble. By altering such a condition, or if that is beyond his power, adjusting himself to it, the illness will gradually disappear.

There are times, however, when a man finds the difficulties of life too great to bear in their fullness, and unconsciously seeks escape from the responsibility of dealing with more than he can stand. This fear of the burden of living can interfere with the flow of vitality at the mento-emotional level and so bring about some chronic physical ailment which will lessen his everyday responsibilities, and relieve him of his more subtle fears. Such an illness can only be cured when he has grown in strength sufficiently to face life's problems in their totality. Until that time arrives, no method of treatment will cure him, though it may bring some degree of relief.

There is another factor to be borne in mind in cases of chronic ill-health, especially when it occurs early in life and its probable causes cannot be found. In such an instance, many people feel that the forces of reaction which brought about the present illness probably had their origin in a previous existence where circumstances were such that the process of readjustment did not have sufficient time to complete its work, and so had to be continued in the present life.

The time taken for an illness of this kind to be cured may take anything from a few months to a whole lifetime, depending on the magnitude of the original forces of disharmony which were generated. The treatment, however, will still be the same as if those forces had had their origin in the present incarnation, though they will probably be more deeply-seated, and so more difficult to eradicate.

There is no panacea for ill-health

We see therefore that the process of healing is the relieving
of these obstructions, and is not dependent on any particular
system such as homeopathy, allopathy, or osteopathy. Any
treatment, whether orthodox or unorthodox, which will
bring about this release of vitality at the required level in a
particular case, will also bring about a healing result, provided the patient is willing to be cured deep down within
himself, and gives his co-operation.

The causes of disease can be placed under three main
headings:

1. *Accidents and Mistakes:* when something harmful is done
inadvertently.
2. *Ignorance:* probably the greatest cause of all, due to the
limitations of the mind with its lack of wisdom.
3. *Fear:* when appearing as a normal function, and without
exaggeration, is essentially protective and beneficent. But
when it is the result of ignorance, it tends to grow out of all
proportion, causing vital restriction and tension at the
emotional level, which in turn is reflected into the physical
body, bringing about disorders of various systems and
organs. Paralysis and various forms of heart strain are common examples, as are probably all neuroses.

In all these cases there is a common belief that one can
escape from the law of cause and effect by paying a chemist
or doctor to supply a medicament which will neutralise all
evil consequences. Such a belief is illusory, for all the remedies can do is to ease symptoms, not remove the results
of one's actions.

The frequent refusal of Man to accept responsibility for

his own actions is well illustrated by the person who deludes himself that his overweight and breathing difficulties are due to some capriciousness of Nature, and so willingly goes to a nursing home to be starved for the fee of thirty guineas a week, rather than admit his responsibility and do it at home for nothing!

Relief is more common than cure

Thus it will be seen that the healer is often restricted by the patient's attitude of mind as to how much help he can give, and has to be satisfied with giving some degree of relief, rather than bringing about a radical cure. Even the great healer of the New Testament who was ever ready to help suffering humanity recognised this limitation, never trying to force his curative powers on the sick, but said to everyone in need, 'I stand at the door and knock'. Thereafter it was the patient himself who had to do the initial opening.

In all matters of therapy one great fact must constantly be borne in mind: that it is Nature which does the actual healing; Man can merely ease Nature's way by co-operating with her, just as a gardener creates the best conditions of soil and environment for his plants to grow to the most perfect expression of what is inherent in them. But however hard he may try, he cannot create a new rose or lily from chemicals and soil.

The greatest of surgeons, performing a very delicate operation, does not cure the patient but simply prepares the ground, by removing diseased tissues or re-adjusting those which are displaced, and so leaving them in the most suitable condition for Nature to carry out her healing processes.

There are various ways in which a physician can help his patient. Sometimes by simple advice, but much more often by sympathetic and compassionate understanding. Such an attitude brings about an atmosphere of harmony on all levels of consciousness, enabling the sufferer to relax inwardly and often release some of the tension causing his illness, without realising what has happened. But more than this, the healer will have created a bridge between himself and the patient along which the healer's own harmonising forces can travel to the sufferer and reinforce the latter's curative powers.

The sympathetic bridge

This sympathetic bridge between doctor and patient is probably the most important factor in personal healing of any kind.

It inspires faith in the patient, and enhances the effect of any physical remedy that may be used, whether the latter has useful powers of its own as in medicines, massage, radiant heat and things of like nature, or in itself is useless but is believed by both to be efficacious. It is this sympathetic bridge-factor which sometimes appears to cause a useless remedy to bring about a cure when a more reliable remedy has failed. The healing power being not in the remedy used, but in the sympathetic understanding created, and the positive desire to help on the part of the healer. This enables the latter to help on the subtler planes of consciousness, and also makes of him a channel for some of Nature's healing forces to pass through to the patient.

Since this sincere wish to help can act equally well at a distance once the bridge of sympathy has been established, and the patient fully wishes to co-operate, the process can be carried on continuously and the results are often spectacular.

It can now be seen why the same ailment may appear to be

hen we consider common remedies in use today we
that many of them come under the category of relievers
ain and distress, rather than methods of cure, and in
ing their usefulness it is most important to avoid non-
itur conclusions, by testing each remedy over and over
1.

power of suggestion

power of suggestion in Man is highly developed, as
y witch doctor or advertiser of commercial products is
l aware, and it is a common experience that when a new
hod of treatment is put on the market, it always has
erous successes in its early days, even though at a later
e it may be found to be useless or even harmful.

n interesting experiment illustrating this principle was
e by the College of General Practitioners a little while
in connection with plantar warts, those most annoying
painful nodules which school children often get in the
es of their feet. They are not at all serious, but very in-
acitating.

One hundred and twenty people of various ages, suffering
m plantar warts (veruccas) were divided into three equal
ups. The first group was given formalin lotion to apply
ly (this being the favourite treatment at the time); the
ond group was given a lotion to apply daily, consisting of
in water; and the third group was given an inert tablet to
e daily. They were not told the nature of their respective
medies and were asked to continue treatment for six weeks
d then return for examination. At the subsequent
amination it was found that 60% had recovered in each
oup. And so one is forced to conclude that in this par-
cular experiment either the power of suggestion or the

cured in one case by the use of a box which is supposed to
radiate health; in another by a drug; in another by an inert
tablet, and in a fourth by prayer.

The remedy used may be simply a dramatic means of
gaining the faith and co-operation of the patient, or it may
in addition have some curative or alleviating action in itself
such as the application of warmth, or an injection of a pain-
relieving chemical.

Sometimes the remedies have to be administered in
stages as when dealing with a severe emotional conflict. In
such a case it may be impossible to make a sympathetic
rapport with the patient owing to his preoccupying agitation, until he has first of all been given a sedative for its
purely drug action. Then when he is calmer it will be
possible to communicate with him and proceed with his
deeper treatment. If a cure results, the patient is quite likely
to be mistakenly led into thinking that the success of his
treatment was due to the drug that was used rather than the
resolution of his emotional difficulties.

Dangers of non-sequitur reasoning

This non-sequitur reasoning is extremely common in health
matters, and has to be guarded against with the utmost
diligence when seeking the true causes of illnesses, and their
most suitable treatments. There is a great temptation to
jump to general conclusions from a single success, especially
when the treatment has been a little unusual.

Chronic diseases particularly lend themselves to this
fallacy when a number of remedies have failed and a final
one seems to succeed.

If we take, for example, a chronic skin disease like
psoriasis for which there is no known medical cure, but only

medical alleviation. It is a distressing disease aesthetically, for although not painful or infectious, large, dry, scaly patches appear on the arms, legs and body, and last anything from a few weeks to a few years. It has one redeeming feature, however, in that sooner or later it usually disappears spontaneously.

It does not take much imagination to realise how frustrated a young person of either sex must feel on being unable to go swimming or sunbathing or playing tennis, and in the case of a woman, unable to wear evening dress. A young girl suffering from psoriasis, and having tried orthodox remedies without success, is likely to turn to magazine advertisements and quack remedies for help. When these in turn fail she is likely to feel desperate. If at that time it should happen that a gipsy meets her and promises to cure her for a small remuneration, one would not be surprised if she jumped at the chance. Supposing the gipsy then tells her with great seriousness that she is to put a spot of honey, which *must* be heather honey, on the rim of her left ear when going to bed each night, and that she is then to go to sleep on her right side, and that in a little while the skin will become normal, she would almost certainly do as she was told.

If, to her delight and amazement, the psoriasis disappeared during the next three or four weeks it would be natural if she gave entire credit to the gipsy for her cure. Yet what would actually have happened is that the disease had run its course and would have disappeared at that time in any case, whether treated or not, but it is unlikely that anyone would ever be able to convince that girl that the honey had nothing to do with it, especially when a particular honey had been recommended, for as Poobah remarked in *The Mikado*, the

introduction of such a detail 'is intended to similitude to an otherwise bald and unconv

It can now be seen that the work of t threefold. In the first place he tries to cre rapport with the patient, and secondly dis the patient's consciousness of the causal ob exact nature. His third task is to help the pa to resolve it by understanding and acceptin

This as a rule is a very difficult process time so that his immediate concern is to allev discomfort caused by the ailment.

Because of the difficulties of everyday life tion on the relief of unpleasant symptoms is t of treatment today, and it is only when the p the time, and is willing to give his full co- spirit of optimism, that the deeper causes of c can be dealt with, and a complete cure brou

Nature—the real healer

Lastly, the therapist uses his knowledge and Nature—the real Healer—to have the best p tions for her work of reconstruction.

These three factors are so intimately connecte in one helps the others. Even the simple trea pleasant symptoms will often enable the patien his mind and personality more clearly than he distracted by suffering.

In such a case, the administration of a powe such as morphia, though poisonous, may do far in the early stages than more delicate and refine which would fail while the patient was wracked in a state of severe mental agitation.

natural rate of spontaneous recovery was responsible for the cures, but not the remedy.

Of course, many remedies do have alleviating properties of their own, and are useful for relieving the symptoms of everyday minor illness, but one must be careful to bear in mind that a treatment is not more efficacious because it is mysterious, or unusual.

A sprained ankle is better treated with a cold compress and perhaps gentle massage, than with coloured light administered by a clairvoyant!

Lack of prejudice essential

It is all a matter of common sense, and the willingness to use any remedy one thinks is best in all the circumstances.

It is also quite fallacious to believe that a particularly favoured system is better than all others, because by doing so the patient may be denied the fullest degree of help to which he is entitled.

And so it seems fairly safe to conclude that in all cases of illness that are really cured, it is the patient himself, working in co-operation with Nature, and often with the assistance of others, who actually brings about the resolution of his own ailment. Without his co-operation and desire to get well, all methods of healing will fail. On the other hand, if for any of these reasons it is not possible to bring about a complete cure, it is usually possible to give him considerable relief, and make his life much happier and easier.

Fortunately for all of us there are forces in Nature which continually work towards health and harmony throughout the biological kingdom. Sometimes these harmonising forces are directed to us through the compassion of our fellow-men, at other times they well up within us from the depths of our being, but however they arrive we can take heart from the fact that they are always at work constructively, helping to reduce suffering and bring about regeneration at any level where disorder and disease exist.

Hypnogogic experiences and the attention centre

During a recent attack of gastro-enteritis, a member of the Science Group found himself with no desire whatever to read or to be entertained in any way. He then recalled a passing comment by a friend to the effect that she could easily see non-physical pictures projected, as she believed, from within on to the outer wall of her 'aura'. She dismissed this faculty as of no consequence.

It nevertheless seemed an amusing thing to try under the circumstances, and success came almost at once. It was assumed that the pictures were conjured up from the unconscious mind by that indwelling intelligence we call 'George' (the mental elemental of theosophical literature). This direct experience of the amazing speed and artistic ability of his 'unconscious Dramatisation' was most instructive. But in addition a few experiments led to the discovery of several useful things at first hand.

At first a few geometrical designs were seen dimly, then what looked like crystal patterns. Soon, as the interest quickened, pictures appeared with increasing rapidity and brightness. These included scenes, chemical engineering plant, figures and faces as well as designs. They faded and were replaced after a few moments. If one looked away the picture stayed where it was (unlike an after-image), and another might be waiting in a different field of view. The pictures sometimes changed, often for the worse. The beautiful face of a child would quickly change through slut

to old crone; other faces assumed a caricature aspect before
fading. A few pictures were definitely unwelcome. The
pictures were seldom recognisable as actual memories, but
all could have been based on material in the subconscious.
One in particular was quite clearly based on a time-lapse
sequence on the crystallisation of vitamin B_{12}, which had
been prepared for a film. In this sequence one crystal breaks
away from the cluster and floats off in the mother-liquor,
and this event was reproduced in the growing crystal
pattern that was seen.

The attention centre

These early experiments were in daylight, and it was noticed
that the picture persisted with half-open eyes (still seen
apparently through the eyelids) but usually vanished on
opening the eyes fully. A few of the brighter ones persisted
for a moment as if drawn on the ceiling, with eyes fully open
in dull daylight. The pictures could be dismissed from view
not only by opening the eyes, but also in another fashion,
namely, by starting to think about something. Merely
readying the attention as if to think sufficed, even without
formulating a problem. This observation gave an opportunity to study the working of what might be called the
'attention centre'. Its operation is evidently the same as the
act of concentration, the first step in meditation. Annie
Besant mentions somewhere that concentration is signalled
by a sensation in the pineal gland 'like an ant creeping'.
This sensation was experienced, though accompanied perhaps by slight involuntary muscular movements in the head.
It was found that this 'attention centre' could be switched on
merely by intention (provided it was genuine and not half-
hearted) and the change was signalled both by the 'creeping'

sensation and disappearance of visual pictures. Relaxation switched it off again, and pictures reappeared. It seemed, however, that the switch tended to stick in the 'on' position when there was tension with resultant insomnia.

That evening, for relaxation, a B.B.C. film was watched of Russian circuses on T.V. On retiring, very tired but over-stimulated, the pictures reappeared with increased brilliance and variety. 'George's' repertoire and technique improved, and he now drew liberally and imaginatively on the circus scenes: the impression was obtained that he must spend most of his spare time sketching, whereas in waking consciousness there was no such inclination or ability. Some pictures now appeared in colour; some were animated instead of static. Now in the dark it made no difference whether the eyes were closed or open, and getting to sleep was a real problem. The persistent ever-changing picture gallery could now only be dismissed by switching on the 'attention centre'—but sleep is impossible while it is 'on'. In fact very little sleep was obtained that night.

With a few exceptions, these pictures had a flat 2D quality like sketches drawn on a canvas. With eyes open they appeared as if on the walls or ceiling, but with eyes closed they sometimes appeared closer, even on the pillow beside one. This impression of varying distance was quite unmistakable, but it may well be asked how such an impression could be formed in the absence of reference objects: the answer is probably that one was conscious of a change in focus of the eyes. It can be argued there was no real evidence that etheric vision or any other type of temporary clair-voyance was involved at all; the pictures could have been 'inserted' at any point in the long sequence between an image on the retina and the event in consciousness. All that can be said is, the impression of 'seeing' was extremely strong and vivid and the nature of the experience entirely different from the normal one of 'seeing in the mind's eye' either a recalled or imagined scene. It is important to note that the writer has a non-visual imagination, and any pictures conjured up in the mind's eye are vague and fleeting in the extreme; these 'visual' pictures on the contrary were clear-cut, detailed and vivid. Moreover they came unbidden in unpredictable array, and showed little response to will or imagination.

The 'sketches' continued the next day during moments of relaxation. Two near-East desert village scenes in golden tints were specially memorable—seen while lying in the morning bath with bright sunlight streaming through the window on to the eyelids. By this time their persistence was worrying and beginning to suggest perpetual sleeplessness ahead. A direct appeal to 'George' to lay off was unavailing, so a policy was initiated of instantly dismissing every picture, by opening the eyes momentarily during daylight and operating the 'attention centre' after dark. The next day only a few pictures were seen and subsequently the phenomenon virtually ceased.

The experience afforded a critical test of one's ability to be aware through two channels simultaneously. Without losing the picture one could think lightly and descriptively about it: or could perhaps have described it aloud to another person. Alternatively music or even conversation could be listened to in a rather vague background fashion—but the moment definite attention was given to any of these, the picture vanished. This was a real object lesson on the difference between passive diffuse reception of incoming sense signals, and actively going out to meet them with focused attention. Of course, once the attention centre is 'on', it can be switched with great rapidity from one object to another, or from one sense channel to another, giving the illusion of being able to attend to several things simultaneously.

Cause of the vision

It is impossible to determine the cause of these remarkable experiences. The deliberate invitation to 'George' to stage his display could hardly have been the sole cause; perhaps etheric vision or some other latent faculty was intensified by the illness, or more specifically by some toxin elaborated by the infecting organism? It is possible that the sulphaguanidine that was being taken contributed, though there were no such experiences on a previous occasion when it was prescribed. Perhaps more than one factor was involved. Since recovery, brief periods of deliberate watching have yielded no repetition of the phenomenon.

The sceptical will doubtless dismiss these visions as products of a disordered imagination, due to illness. There is a sense in which this diagnosis must be accepted; nevertheless it is quite definite that they were not the result of *conscious* imagination; also that the mode of presentation was unique in the writer's experience.

How do these experiences compare with others recorded? Why moreover does this kind of thing not occur more frequently—or does it indeed, but the victims keep quiet about it? These visions may well tally with those seen during sensory deprivation experiments. They are presumably not like those induced by hallucinogenic drugs, because they had no emotional content; there was no sense of exhilaration, fear or depression, though this could be due to a cold-

blooded, self-analytical attitude. Are these the kind of
visions that would be seen by a would-be medium 'sitting
for development'? This seems quite likely, in which event
the medium's visions might be purely internal, i.e. arising
from the subconscious and having no contact at all with any
part of the psychic world outside. One has no illusions as to
the value of these particular visions. They were of the same
calibre as dream memories or the day-dreams and fantasies
of an idle mind. At the best, they might afford some insight into the state of one's own subconscious mind.

Previous accounts of hypnogogic experiences

Up to this point, the account was written without reference
to any previous work. Its circulation within the Science
Group resulted in the writer's being shown a copy of the
Proceedings of the Society for Psychical Research for May
1925, devoted to a review of hypnogogic phenomena.
Many of these experiences tally remarkably closely with the
ones here described. The following additional notes include
comparisons with this published work and a summary of a
discussion by the Science Group. It is perhaps unfortunate
that the writer started with preconceived notions concerning
the nature of his visions; however, these ideas tallied broadly
with those of most other members of the Group.

The phenomenon appears to be less uncommon than was
supposed; some writers estimate that one person in three has
had the experience at some time in his life, most probably in
childhood. Nearly all the observations here recorded can be
matched by one or other of the many examples quoted in
the S.P.R. *Journal*, though naturally they did not cover the
entire gamut of recorded varieties of the experience.

The term 'hypnogogic phenomena', coined well over

100 years ago, is meant to imply that the visions are seen during the brief period of semiconsciousness just before falling asleep. (Images seen just at wakening are called hypnopompic phenomena.) Although it was supposed previously that these experiences did not fall into either category, because most of them occurred while wide awake, it transpired after critical reading of the S.P.R. material that this was also true for many of the examples quoted. Perhaps an essential condition (though not of course the only one) is a state of complete relaxation. Most mentally active people seldom achieve this state until they *are* nearly asleep; however, illness in this case had induced a lethargic, relaxed, but not sleepy condition. One wonders whether the extensive use of sedatives and tranquillising drugs may not sometimes defeat its object by turning the patient into an involuntary seer. In several, but by no means all, of the recorded cases, the visions occurred during illness. Nearly all the visions were unrecognised, but known faces or scenes appeared occasionally to some seers. In only a few instances did the images respond to will or imagination, either at initiation or dismissal.

The S.P.R. account has little to say that is useful about the causes of the phenomena. Many observers are able to differentiate clearly between memory-images, imagination-images or visualisations, entoptic flashes arising within the eye, and hypnagogic pictures; and the latter are usually not fuzzy but exceptionally clear-cut and distinct, often miniature in scale, and sometimes showing even more detail than normal eyesight could provide. In other words, there is a real phenomenon in need of explanation. Some people believe the scenes to be those of past lives; others believe them to be premonitory; others again suppose them to be clairvoyant visions of actual events occurring elsewhere. Naturally these unsupported beliefs cannot be accepted as evidence. The term 'hypnogogic agent' used by the reviewer is significant as implying the operation of an intelligent agent other than the conscious mind in creating the pictures. She quotes Sir John Herschel's speaking, in 1858, of 'a thought, an intelligence, working within our own organisation distinct from that of our own personality'.

In our discussion the suggestion of material in the subconscious mind being manipulated at that level and thrown up into consciousness was generally accepted, but several members thought that external material could also contribute to the pictures. The fact that attention caused their disappearance suggested that they came through the sympathetic system. One member doubted if the eye or 'etheric eye' was really involved. He thought the visions were brought more directly to conscious notice and the eye tricked, as it were, into supposing that it was the agent, even to the extent of making changes of focus to correspond with the apparent distances of the images. Another member remarked: 'Instead of regarding psychic faculties of perception as extensions of the physical ones, I regard the physical perceptive powers as the lowest extension of the psychic faculties and the most restricted in scope.'

THE THEOSOPHICAL PUBLISHING HOUSE

Wheaton, Ill., U.S.A.

Madras, India   London, England

Publishers of a wide range of titles on many
subjects including:

Mysticism

Yoga

Meditation

Extrasensory Perception

Religions of the World

Asian Classics

Reincarnation

The Human Situation

Theosophy

Distributors for the Adyar Library Series of Sanskrit
Texts, Translations and Studies

The Theosophical Publishing House, Wheaton,
Illinois, is also the publisher of

QUEST BOOKS

Many titles from our regular clothbound list in
attractive paperbound editions

*For a complete descriptive list of all Quest Books
write to:*

QUEST BOOKS
P.O. Box 270, Wheaton, Ill. 60187

cured in one case by the use of a box which is supposed to radiate health; in another by a drug; in another by an inert tablet, and in a fourth by prayer.

The remedy used may be simply a dramatic means of gaining the faith and co-operation of the patient, or it may in addition have some curative or alleviating action in itself such as the application of warmth, or an injection of a pain-relieving chemical.

Sometimes the remedies have to be administered in stages as when dealing with a severe emotional conflict. In such a case it may be impossible to make a sympathetic rapport with the patient owing to his preoccupying agitation, until he has first of all been given a sedative for its purely drug action. Then when he is calmer it will be possible to communicate with him and proceed with his deeper treatment. If a cure results, the patient is quite likely to be mistakenly led into thinking that the success of his treatment was due to the drug that was used rather than the resolution of his emotional difficulties.

Dangers of non-sequitur reasoning

This non-sequitur reasoning is extremely common in health matters, and has to be guarded against with the utmost diligence when seeking the true causes of illnesses, and their most suitable treatments. There is a great temptation to jump to general conclusions from a single success, especially when the treatment has been a little unusual.

Chronic diseases particularly lend themselves to this fallacy when a number of remedies have failed and a final one seems to succeed.

If we take, for example, a chronic skin disease like psoriasis for which there is no known medical cure, but only

R

medical alleviation. It is a distressing disease aesthetically, for although not painful or infectious, large, dry, scaly patches appear on the arms, legs and body, and last anything from a few weeks to a few years. It has one redeeming feature, however, in that sooner or later it usually disappears spontaneously.

It does not take much imagination to realise how frustrated a young person of either sex must feel on being unable to go swimming or sunbathing or playing tennis, and in the case of a woman, unable to wear evening dress. A young girl suffering from psoriasis, and having tried orthodox remedies without success, is likely to turn to magazine advertisements and quack remedies for help. When these in turn fail she is likely to feel desperate. If at that time it should happen that a gipsy meets her and promises to cure her for a small remuneration, one would not be surprised if she jumped at the chance. Supposing the gipsy then tells her with great seriousness that she is to put a spot of honey, which *must* be heather honey, on the rim of her left ear when going to bed each night, and that she is then to go to sleep on her right side, and that in a little while the skin will become normal, she would almost certainly do as she was told.

If, to her delight and amazement, the psoriasis disappeared during the next three or four weeks it would be natural if she gave entire credit to the gipsy for her cure. Yet what would actually have happened is that the disease had run its course and would have disappeared at that time in any case, whether treated or not, but it is unlikely that anyone would ever be able to convince that girl that the honey had nothing to do with it, especially when a particular honey had been recommended, for as Poobah remarked in *The Mikado*, the introduction of such a detail 'is intended to give artistic veri-similitude to an otherwise bald and unconvincing narrative!'

It can now be seen that the work of the ideal healer is threefold. In the first place he tries to create a sympathetic rapport with the patient, and secondly discover the level in the patient's consciousness of the causal obstruction and its exact nature. His third task is to help the patient, if possible, to resolve it by understanding and accepting it.

This as a rule is a very difficult process and takes a long time so that his immediate concern is to alleviate the pain and discomfort caused by the ailment.

Because of the difficulties of everyday life this concentration on the relief of unpleasant symptoms is the chief method of treatment today, and it is only when the patient can spare the time, and is willing to give his full co-operation in a spirit of optimism, that the deeper causes of chronic sickness can be dealt with, and a complete cure brought about.

Nature—the real healer

Lastly, the therapist uses his knowledge and skill to assist Nature—the real Healer—to have the best possible conditions for her work of reconstruction.

These three factors are so intimately connected that success in one helps the others. Even the simple treatment of unpleasant symptoms will often enable the patient to examine his mind and personality more clearly than he could when distracted by suffering.

In such a case, the administration of a powerful sedative such as morphia, though poisonous, may do far more good in the early stages than more delicate and refined treatments which would fail while the patient was wracked with pain or in a state of severe mental agitation.

When we consider common remedies in use today we find that many of them come under the category of relievers of pain and distress, rather than methods of cure, and in judging their usefulness it is most important to avoid non-sequitur conclusions, by testing each remedy over and over again.

The power of suggestion

The power of suggestion in Man is highly developed, as every witch doctor or advertiser of commercial products is well aware, and it is a common experience that when a new method of treatment is put on the market, it always has numerous successes in its early days, even though at a later date it may be found to be useless or even harmful.

An interesting experiment illustrating this principle was done by the College of General Practitioners a little while ago in connection with plantar warts, those most annoying and painful nodules which school children often get in the soles of their feet. They are not at all serious, but very incapacitating.

One hundred and twenty people of various ages, suffering from plantar warts (veruccas) were divided into three equal groups. The first group was given formalin lotion to apply daily (this being the favourite treatment at the time); the second group was given a lotion to apply daily, consisting of plain water; and the third group was given an inert tablet to take daily. They were not told the nature of their respective remedies and were asked to continue treatment for six weeks and then return for examination. At the subsequent examination it was found that 60% had recovered in each group. And so one is forced to conclude that in this particular experiment either the power of suggestion or the